THE UNIVERSITY OF
WINCHESTER

Martial Rose Library
Tel: 01962 827306

To be returned on or before the day marked above, subject to recall.

Also by Christos Yannaras

Elements of Faith

On the Absence and Unknowability of God

Orthodoxy and the West

Person and Eros

Postmodern Metaphysics

The Freedom of Morality

Variations on the Song of Songs

CHRISTOS YANNARAS

RELATIONAL ONTOLOGY

Translated by
Norman Russell

HOLY CROSS ORTHODOX PRESS
Brookline, Massachusetts

Published by Holy Cross Orthodox Press
50 Goddard Avenue
Brookline, Massachusetts 02445

ISBN-13 978-1-935317-19-7
ISBN-10 1-935317-19-9

Originally published in Greek as *Ontologia tēs scheseōs*, Ikaros, Athens, 2004.

On the cover: Francis Picabia (1879–1953), *Dances at the Spring*, 1912. © ARS,
NY. Oil on canvas, the Louise and Walter Arensberg Collection, 1950.
Location: Philadelphia Museum of Art, Philadelphia, Pennsylvania, USA.
Photo Credit: The Philadelphia Museum of Art / Art Resource, NY.

Library of Congress Cataloging-in-Publication Data

Giannaras, Chrestos, 1935-
[Ontologia tes scheses. English]
 Relational ontology / Christos Yannaras ; translated by Norman Russell.
   p. cm.
 Includes bibliographical references and index.
 ISBN-13: 978-1-935317-19-7
 ISBN-10: 1-935317-19-9
 1. Relation (Philosophy) I. Title.
 B836.G5313 2011
 111--dc22
                                                        2011010168

*Jeder Satz, den ich schreibe, meint immer schon das Ganze,
also immer wieder dasselbe und es sind gleichsam nur
Ansichten eines Gegenstandes unter verschiedenen Winkeln
betrachtet.*

Every proposition that I write always means the whole, and
is thus the same thing over and over again. It is as if they
are only views of a single object seen from various angles.

—Ludwig Wittgenstein
Vermischte Bemerkungen, 1930

Contents

Relation in Our Linguistic Code

1 Can we speak of a *relational ontology*—in Greek, an *ontology of relation*? Is this an expression consistent with the semantic content or the meaning of the words constituting it, an expression consistent—also as a structured group of meanings—with linguistic logic?

1.1   The reply to this question will be affirmative if we can prove that the fact signified by the word *relation* may (in certain circumstances) have an *ontological* content, that *relation* may constitute an ontological fact—that is, a *mode* of existence or even a *foundational* fact of existence.

1.1.1   Such a possibility would seem to be excluded by the semantic content (the meaning) that normal language (the language of everyday communication) bestows on the term *relation*: relation presupposes that the factors which constitute it—the *terms* or *constituents* of the fact of relation, the parts related to each other—actually exist.

1.1.2   In the empirical logic expressed by our everyday language, something first *exists* and is then *related* to, or comes into relation with, something else—something that is already existent.

1.1.3   It is not possible for us to understand a relation before or apart from the terms that constitute it. We cannot define it as an autonomous existential fact or define existence as a relation, by-passing the subject (i.e., the bearer) of existence. Our linguistic logic, the semantics of our common experience, necessarily pre-supposes a subject, or bearer, of existence and presupposes relation as a fact that follows.

1.2   Every existent being—that is, every subject, or bearer, of ex-istence—is identified by the senses and the intellect as an actually existing *definitive*[1] given, a given which precedes any eventuality that it should constitute a term or constituent of relation. But at the same time, common experience confirms that every being ex-ists only as a coherent combination of relations, only as situated within a network of relations. Common experience confirms that what every being *is* emerges as a result of relations between a host of causal factors.

1.2.1   The relations (i.e., the modes and kinds of relation) between the smallest discernible quantities (quanta) of natural energy, force, electrical charge, and so forth, constitute the elementary particles of matter and every form of material reality.[2] From a particular kind of relation of two living beings—the sexual union—a new existence comes into being: an existential fact is established, an otherness of the existential fact. Moreover, the continuation, or maintenance, of the existence of living beings presupposes a direct organic relation-ship with the natural environment (the reception of oxygen, food, and drink). Finally, from their relationship with reality's material givens, human beings, too, produce existential otherness (of a cre-ative kind) through each of their activities connected with making and constructing.

1.2.2   We signify the reality of the world as the consequence and the totality of activated relations by using either the images of the cosmogonic myths or the language of the modern sciences. We sit-uate both universal-natural becoming and human-social becoming within a set of relations. Consequently, we speak of relation as the mode by which something that exists does so.[3]

1.2.3   Yet we constantly speak of relations that are presubjective constituents of relations: existential realities connected with the given factors or terms of relation. We refer to relation not as if it were a non-presupposed existential fact, not as if it were an actual realization of an existential fact. Consequently, in our discussion, the term *relational ontology* remains unjustified both logically and pragmatically.

Methodological Boundary Markers

2 The *ontological problem* is the name we give to our endeavor to account for the being of existent things, the *logos* of beings. We seek an answer to questions about the *cause* and *purpose* of the existential fact; we look for the "reason" (*logos*) for the existence of that which exists.

2.1   Interwoven with the ontological problem is also uncertainty about our very ability to seek the cause and purpose (the *logos*) of the existence of existent things—uncertainty about the particularity of human reason. What is the cause of the *rationality* of human beings? What is its purpose? Does rationality (*logikotēs*) have a reason (*logos*)?

2.1.1   Is the human capacity for rational thought a sufficient basis for the interpretation of the existential fact? Can it provide an answer to the ontological problem? Our uncertainty about the cause and purpose seems to belong to the given mode in which our rational capacity as human beings functions. Does this mode suffice to interpret the entire reality of existent things and of being itself? Is there a given correspondence between the whole of what constitutes reality and the mode by which human beings perceive or apprehend or recognize this reality? Or should we concede that humanity's capacity for rational thought is simply an isolated coincidence in the biological evolution of mammals—a product of the instinct for self-preservation—within a nonrational universe?

2.1.2   In every event, the human capacity for rational thought is manifested as a function of relation (of the infant to its mother, etc.), not as an innate given property (like, for example, the desire for food). Of course, human rationality is founded on biological presuppositions, but these constitute only the necessary conditions for rationality; they do not guarantee its capacity.

The transition from the functions of perception to the fact of subjective *self-knowledge* or *self-consciousness*, where the capacity for reason is recapitulated, is not an innate (functionally or biologically automatic) property.

2.1.3   The presuppositions for the formation of subjective self-knowledge or self-consciousness are primarily relational (i.e., functions of relations), not primarily biological (i.e., products of instincts). The confirmation of this is provided by the character of existential otherness, through which subjective self-consciousness is activated or manifested—a character of comparative dissimilarity, of uniqueness.

2.1.4   The otherness of the rational subject is an existential fact: it is activated or manifested as a uniqueness that is not subject to general, common predeterminations, which belong to the essence or nature. That is to say, the otherness of the rational subject is activated or manifested as an existential fact or a product of indeterminacy, or *freedom*.

2.2   Mythological, religious, and philosophical traditions represent a variety of responses to the ontological (along with the anthropological) problem. By what reliable means—by what method or criteria—can we distinguish credible responses from those that lack credibility? Are the methods and criteria of correct logical thought (i.e., reliable knowledge), which are valid for the propositions of natural science, also valid for propositions relating to the ontological question?

2.2.1   The propositions of natural science are inferred from empirical convictions that have been subjected to common verification. And they are expressed in a linguistic set of symbols that gives shape to modes, forms, and schemata that refer to processes and sequences corresponding to those of the empirical convictions. Modes, forms, and schemata of linguistic expression are created that refer to and represent causal connections, inductive and deductive conclusions, compelling sequences of meaning—language determines how we approach the specific "state" of what is given.

2.2.2   We also use the power language gives us to refer to empirical convictions in order to demonstrate (intellectually and critically) possible interpretations of the existential fact. *Logic* and *correct reasoning* are the names we give to the rules of *correct intellection* shaped by human experience, rules which are indispensable for understanding (in Greek, *syn-ennoēsis*, literally "a coming together in the mind"). That is to say, these are the names we give to the functional (accessible to all and persuasive to all) determination of the necessary and sufficient conditions for identifying empirical convictions and referring to them.

One of the ways in which we can respond to the ontological question is to trust the rules of correct intellection, which are generally accepted as a result of common experience.

2.2.3   An exaggerated confidence in correct reasoning—known by expressions such as *intellectualism, rational dogmatism,* and *instrumental rationalism*—in close association with the historical evolution of the Western European religious and philosophical traditions, has been the subject of critical discussion in a large number of works.[1] But this exaggerated confidence does not invalidate the way the *dialectic method of syllogisms* functions.[2]

2.3   There also exists the so-called *mystical* approach to the interpretation of the *logos* (i.e., cause and purpose) of the existence of existent things. This is the approach that does not give priority to intellectual convictions—that is, to rational deduction or to judgments inferred from consequences arising from the utilitarian understanding of syllogisms. The mystical approach relies on the obviousness (the self-evidence, self-manifestation[3]) of the *logos*-meaning as it emerges from the experience of participation in the manifestations of the existential fact. It cannot be judged as a method (or as an epistemic consequence flowing from a coherent method), for it represents an epistemological undertaking that is self-defining and beyond conceptual determinations—and consequently beyond the powers of linguistic expression. Mystical experience does not entirely renounce its linguistic expression, but it attempts to express itself indirectly through allegories, poetic images, and metaphors.

2.3.1   The language of allegory, poetic image, and metaphor is clearly not subject to any kind of apodictic argumentation. It is, however, subject to experiential verification: one can try to participate in the experiential practice—the effort of *praxis*—that marks the obviousness or self-evidence of mystical knowledge.

2.3.2   That is why it is also extremely difficult for anyone to distinguish (even when—or chiefly when—dealing with his or her subjective experiences) mystical knowledge from psychological delusion or autosuggestion, to differentiate between mystical experience and the infrangible "certainties" that are created in a person by what psychoanalysts call overcompensation for repressed needs or desires that are buried in the unconscious.[4]

2.4   Both the intellectualist approach and the mystical approach to the interpretation (*logos*) of the existential fact presuppose a specific *individual* capacity in human beings: the capacity for intellectual operations, the capacity for mystical experience. It is particularly within the context of a specific culture, the Western European (and today, global) way of life, that ontological hermeneutics have remained tied to an individualistic perspective: every attempt to delve into the *logos*-meaning of the existence of existent things has been based on one or another of humanity's individual capabilities, whether given or potential.

2.4.1   The individualistic paths or modes of approaching propositions of ontological hermeneutics are usually either (a) a widely accepted discipline of atomic understanding following the codified method of correct intellection, or (b) a combination of the rational method with the suggestive freedom of allegory, poetic image, and metaphor.

It is perhaps from the mixture of the rationalist and mystical approaches that "the most fundamental confusions" are created, confusions that "the whole of philosophy is full of."[5]

2.4.2   An extreme but nevertheless representative case of "fundamental confusion" is the attempt to approach the problem of ontology using a vague terminology with idealistic, romantic overtones. This terminology, which seems to be of Augustinian provenance, clearly has a psychological (rather than an epistemological) aim. Neither *meaning* nor *experience* is manifested by linguistic signifiers such as: *sense of interiority, depths of the self, clarity of the psyche, interior knowledge, radical interiority, interior vision, shudder of interiority*, and so forth.[6]

2.5   In the case of the Greek philosophical tradition (from the pre-Socratics to the fourteenth century), the ontological problem remains free from subordination to theories of atomic individuality. It stays rooted in the *social* verification of hermeneutic propositions, that is, in the social verification of knowledge: the linguistic signifiers are verified when they refer to a signified experience that is shared in common. That which is shared is true; that which is possessed privately is false.[7] The fact that the experience of everyone coincides in a specific form of expression thus verifies the expression and ensures the correctness of the knowledge conveyed by the understanding of the expression.[8]

2.5.1   The social criterion for the verification of knowledge links the mode by which we know with the mode by which we exist, and the topos of this linking is the struggle to attain *relation*, or *communion*. Truth is that knowledge that is assured by the knowledge of each person (his or her relation with reality) and that is confirmed by a testimony, or a verbal expression, in which all persons coincide—through which all are brought into a relation among themselves and with reality.

2.5.2   The social verification of knowledge links the mode by which we know with the mode by which we exist: it links *truth* with *democracy* and *ecclesia*; it links truth with the common struggle to attain the relations that enable us to share in life. No authenticity, no compelling revelation, guarantees truth *according to reason*. Truth is only achieved through the struggle to attain *relations according to reason*.

2.5.3   Relation is knowledge as immediate experiential assurance, the mode by which we recognize reality.

It is the mode by which we participate in the communion of experiential assurance, the mode by which each person can verify knowledge of reality.

It is the mode by which what we recognize as existent exists, the mode by which existence is both realized and manifested.

2.6   In the context of post-Newtonian epistemology, the apophaticism of the Greek tradition of the theory of knowledge acquires a new importance. We call *apophaticism* (1) the denial that we exhaust knowledge in its formulation; (2) the refusal to identify the understanding of the signifiers with the knowledge of what is signified; and (3) the symbolic character of every epistemic expression: its role in bringing together atomic experiences and embracing them within a common semantic boundary marker, a process which allows epistemic experience to be shared and once shared to be verified.[9]

"Something More" than the Mode of Nature

3 We use the word *relation* with at least two meanings:

The first meaning of *relation* is as a correlation of two or more given, or definitive, beings. The correlation is inferred from a comparison of where the beings are located in space and time, of their forms, and of their quantitative and qualitative differences and characteristics.

The second meaning of *relation* is as an active mode by which the being of existent things is constituted, as is also our knowledge of every existent thing.

3.1   With regard to the second meaning of the word *relation*, the being of water is constituted by a specific quantitative relation between atoms of hydrogen and atoms of oxygen. The way the being of other existent things (whether inanimate or animate) is constituted presupposes relations of a compounded combination of much simpler elements. The *mode* of the relation of whatever elements constitute the being—the mode of their causal combination—determines the *identity* of the being, that which the being *is*.

Certain givens, however, are always presupposed—namely, the simple elements that already exist and that together constitute the being's specific form (the relation giving rise to species). Before the *how* of existence, then, there is the *what* of the underlying matter.

3.1.1   The semantic and linguistic coherence of the term *relational ontology* remains in suspension if we seek in the meaning of *ontology* something more than the location of a mode of existence.

3.2   There are two propositions from different epistemic areas, different fields of experience, which refer to "something more" than locating a mode in the meaning of *relation*.

The first proposition comes from the field of epistemic research in metaphysics—specifically, from the theology of the Christian Church—and declares that "God is love."[1]

The second proposition comes from the experience of clinical psychology and affirms that "the [rational] subject is born in the place of the Other."[2]

3.2.1   In the first proposition, the word *love* clearly refers to a meaning different from that in everyday use. *Love* here does not mean a form or quality of behavior that is usually in evidence in expressions such as to be "full of love," or to "show love," and so forth. In spite of its semiologically given referential (relational) character, the word *love* functions in this particular proposition as a definition: it defines the *is*, the reality of being, before any manifestation of activity or determination of behavior.

3.2.2   This particular proposition refers to the *being* of God, which lies entirely outside humanity's epistemic capabilities. The Christian Church itself affirms, with constant repetition in its liturgical practice, that the God to whom it refers is *inexpressible, inconceivable, invisible, incomprehensible.*[3] At the same time, however, the Church defines the *being* of this God as *love*. Not that God's existence precedes his love, which then follows as a property or a characteristic, not that he first *is* and afterwards loves—rather, the Church declares that what God *is*, his real being, can be defined only as *love*.

3.2.3   In the specific context in which it is given, the statement "God is love" could be a metaphor, an allegory, or an instance of metonymy—the statement is not set within a systematic, logically coherent analysis of the ontological problem. The statement is, however, set within language that Christian speech has shaped from the beginning with the aim of conveying the meaning of ontological definitions. The language of the earliest written sources of the Christian ecclesiastical tradition—of its sacred texts—although not the language of systematic rational analysis, provided the ready-made conceptual material out of which subsequently, in the course of the history of philosophy, a fuller ontological proposition was constructed.

3.3   If, with the definition "God is love" as our starting point, we search for a corresponding definition of what humanity *is*, of the human *being* before any manifestation of activity or determination of behavior, what linguistic formula could we propose that is semiologically consistent with common experience?

I offer this defining proposition: humanity *is* nature with accidents.

3.3.1   *Nature* signifies the given common mode of existence of a uniform species of existent things, of beings of a common species.

Accident signifies a mode of the mode—the partial modal version of the common mode of any nature.[4]

3.3.2   *Humanity is nature with accidents* signifies the following: that which humanity is may be defined as the existential fact of a given (predetermined, not self-generated) *mode*—a mode that differentiates humanity from every other being. In each particular human being, however, the common mode of human nature is realized existentially *with accidents*—that is, with the qualitative or differential characteristics that constitute the uniqueness of each human subject.

3.4   From these two definitions—God *is* love; humanity *is* nature with accidents—we infer (noetically) two senses of the verb *to be*, two existential possibilities.

First, being should have its causal principle in *nature*—in a given, predetermined mode that is not self-generated (and therefore necessary).

Second, being has its causal principle in its own self—it defines itself existentially as freedom from any predetermination; being transcends definitive (natural) atomicity, and it exists as a free disposition toward relation and self-offering. That is, being exists as *love*.

3.4.1   From these two definitions, we infer (noetically) two existential possibilities: the fact of being is constituted either on the basis of nature, or on the basis of relation.

3.4.2   The constitution, or realization, of being on the basis of nature means that material givens—simple chemical elements—are correlated and put together in a specific (again, given) mode, from which emerges every partial species (*eidos*) of that which exists.

Each one of the atomic realizations (*hypostases*) of each species constitutes a unique, dissimilar, and unrepeatable mode of existence of the species.

If the species constitutes a *particularity* of the mode of the realization of being (in comparison with other species), every hypostasized species constitutes a *difference* in the mode of the realization of being (in comparison with the other hypostases of the same species).

3.4.3   In every species, the hypostatic difference is given; it is morphic-functional. Only in humanity is it also operative—that is, creative-productive on account of difference.

3.4.4   Both the particularity of the existential mode that constitutes the *species*, or the specifying difference, and the mode of the difference of hypostasis are realized (constituting an existential fact) on the basis of nature with the presupposition of the material givens of nature, the terms, or blueprints, by which material nature is *activated* existentially. The *logos*–mode of difference of every human hypostasis in particular, however, although realized existentially by the operations (energies) of material nature, is differentiated definitively from the existential constants of the natural operations. The hypostasis constitutes an operative (i.e., creative-productive) differentiality with regard to the modal uniformity of the species, a differentiality that signifies clear margins for a certain freedom from natural necessities.

3.5 From these two definitions—God *is* love; humanity *is* nature with accidents—we infer (noetically) two different existential

possibilities: (1) *uncreated* being, which is free from any predetermination of nature or essence (with the freedom to manifest itself
as *love*: self-volitional, self-transcendent referentiality of self-offering or relation); and (2) *created* being, which is subject to prescriptions that constitute necessities of existential limits, but with some
possibilities of relative freedom, that is to say, of self-transcendent
referentiality, or *relation*.

In the "logical space" that determines the signifier *anthrōpos*
(human being) we also include the possibilities of self-transcending referentiality—relative existential freedom—which are always
made operative (by the natural operations of self-conscious rationality and creative difference) as *relation* or *invitation-to-relation*.

3.5.1 Self-conscious rationality and creative-productive difference mark the boundaries of the possibilities of relative existential
freedom—they are particularities that differentiate the human being from every other existent thing in the world. They make the
human being "superior" (with advantages in terms of existential
capabilities) in comparison with the other existent things (according to our human, rational judgment).

With these particularities of relative freedom, which our experience assures us we have, we build our comparative anagogic ascent to the logical space of the meaning of the word *God*: we receive
God's freedom as absolute and consequently his being as naturally
undetermined (by nature or essence)—that is to say, as uncreated.
Using the possibilities of our linguistic semantics, we say that freedom from nature—relative and therefore also absolute freedom—is
realized existentially as relation, as self-transcending referentiality,
or love.

3.5.2 Self-conscious rationality and the capacity to be creative—
that is, to be productive of difference—are the only qualities of existential freedom that we know. This existential freedom is a freedom
from predeterminations or necessities of nature or essence, and for
that reason we also know its qualities to be realized and manifested
as facts of relation. We judge these qualities as superior to any other
(experientially known) existential possibility and we attribute them
supremely—as absolute existential freedom—to God.

This ascent (*anagōgē*) does not "prove" the existence of God; that which really exists is known by human beings through the experience of relation, not merely as an intellectual concept. Nevertheless, the ascent shapes the linguistic semantics that are (eventually) capable of expressing the historical experience of relation.

3.5.3   We know the *relative* existential freedom of human beings; that is, it is accessible to our experience. Its rational exposition also marks out by antithesis the meaning of the *absolute* existential freedom of God.

3.6   We describe the existential freedom of human beings as *relative*—as limited, moderated, constricted, defective—for two principal reasons.

First, human existence can transcend only some (not all) of the limitations imposed by the necessity or prescriptions of nature. It cannot transcend time, space, decay, death.

Second, because that which each atomic human being *is* is constituted in a prescribed way from specific natural energies, or operations (not from other possible ones), intellection, judgment, imagination, and will are coordinated biological—corruptible and mutable—functions (of the brain).

3.6.1   We speak of humanity's existential *freedom*, which is relative but real, because only humanity realizes the given (by its nature) prescriptions of its existence by a mode of unforeseen difference of otherness.

3.6.2   It is a natural (belonging to the same modality) necessity that humanity should possess intellection, reason, judgment, imagination, and will. Every specific human being, however, thinks, judges, imagines, wills, and expresses himself or herself in a unique, dissimilar, and unrepeatable mode—a mode of unpredictable difference, or otherness, which objectively defies description or delimitation.

3.6.3   Every human being "hypostasizes" the *what* of the given, or common, natural powers (or energies), realizing it existentially, as a modal *how* of a relatively free self-determination.

3.6.4   We speak of humanity's *relative* existential freedom not only because its existential self-determination is tied to given natural powers (or energies), but also because the otherness of self-determination has several factors necessarily imposed upon it—such as heredity, the natural and social environment, historical coincidences, and perhaps others, too.

3.6.5   With the limitations on humanity's existential self-determination as given, we call *freedom* humanity's power (developed or inert, fully present or deficient, but never nugatory) to realize the homotropy, or modal homogeneity, of nature as an otherness of operation.

3.7   The meaning of *otherness* can only be comparative (i.e., morphic) when the *other* is defined in relation to a given homotropy.

In its hypostatic expression, every natural operation (of any natural homotropy) has a specific, or morphic, otherness.

The difference between the homotropy of the natural operation and the otherness of its hypostatic expression is a difference signifying *logos*: natural homotropy signifies the *logos* of the species, and hypostatic otherness signifies the *logos* of the subject.

Both logoi are situated (as is their difference) within humanity's rational (*logikē*) capacity, or the rationality that is accidental to human nature—the mode by which a human being recognizes and signs reality.

3.7.1   The meaning of otherness can be one signifying freedom when the *other* is defined, and confirmed, as an existential detaching of the subject from the limitations, or necessities, of nature.

The only mode accessible to empirical confirmation by which the natural operation, hypostatically expressed, constitutes a fact of (relative) freedom from the limitations, or necessities, of nature is that which we call *relation*—for example, the mode of *language* and the mode of *art*.

3.7.2   The poet through language, the composer through music, the artist through shapes and colors are in relation, for instance, with me—relation that is not bound to the laws of nature (at least not to the laws of time and space). Cavafy and Mozart *exist* for me through the otherness of their hypostatic operations, certainly more vividly than they existed for some neighbor of theirs who could only confirm their physical presence in the years and in the cities in which they lived.

This is a preliminary experiential confirmation (by way of example only) of relative freedom from nature, freedom that is realized as a fact of relation. The rational subject transcends the limitations of nature without abolishing the reality of nature—without abolishing, that is, the operations by which nature exists.

The Difference between Desire and Urge

4 Every living being exists in relational immediacy with the reality that surrounds it.

Relational immediacy, in the case of animate beings, means specific forms of the dependence of the fact of existence on the environment in which the existence is realized. It means taking in oxygen, taking in food and drink, adapting to climatic conditions, being exposed to dangers that threaten survival, and so forth.

4.1   We can describe the relational immediacy of the animate being with the reality that surrounds it as a *vital* relation: this immediacy constitutes the necessary precondition of life for the animate being.

In each of its partial manifestations or realizations, this vital relation has an evident morphic, or comparative, *otherness*: every natural operation expressed hypostatically possesses a morphic-comparative otherness.

In particular, we say that humanity's relation with the environment is also *rational*—that is, *conscious* and *intelligible*—because it recognizes and signs, or communicates, the recognition of the morphic-comparative otherness of every natural operation that is expressed hypostatically.

4.1.1   Humanity's rational relation with the reality that surrounds it also implies the possibility of the relation's self-determination.

18

The self-determination of rationality is not only its rational descriptive location but also the rational location of its causal origin.

4.1.2   The following is a tentative proposition locating the causal origin of rationality.

Observation 1: A human being is born with the natural (i.e., biological) presuppositions of rationality—namely, an exceptionally developed brain—but without the functions of rationality having been brought together, that is, without thought, reason, judgment, imagination, will, and so forth.

Observation 2: The child of a rational human being and the offspring of an irrational animal are born sharing a property in common: the (autonomous) *urge* or *instinct* of *self-preservation*. A distinguishing difference in the human case is that this sovereign instinct of existence is endowed with the particularity of *desire*.

Observation 3: An *urge* could also be indicated linguistically as a stimulus provoked by a need—a stimulus leading to physical and psychological arousal—with the specific aim of a physical operation (e.g., the ingestion of food). A *desire* has the character of a need, but more in the sense of a *demand*; that is to say, desire makes the satisfaction of the need depend upon someone else, to whom the need is addressed as a demand. The natural operation that satisfies the need and is its goal (e.g., the ingestion of food) does not fulfill the desire; the fulfillment of the desire is mediated by the ingestion of food but is not exhausted in the ingestion of food, in the satisfaction of the physical need.

4.1.3   When we say that desire coordinates the need with the demand, we mean that in human beings the need has a referential character. The need "passes over toward" the other opposite us; it is a demand for relation. It is not a demand for some partial operation of relation but rather a demand for universal relation through the natural need, a demand that life should be realized as relation. The desire is a "demande d'amour," as Lacan, for example, would say.[1]

4.1.4   The desire for *life-as-relation* is signified, in the language of post-Freudian psychology, as erotic desire, as *libido*.

4.1.5   The difference between need as urge and need as desire—a difference between the satisfaction of natural need and the demand for relation—seems to be the great leap from the irrational animal to the rational human being, a leap unexplained in evolutionary terms.

4.1.6   In the human infant, the dominant desire for life-as-relation is mediated by the need for food. That is why in the human infant alone, the sensory location of the power to respond to the need for food (the location of the mother's breast) leads not to reactions of a Pavlovian type but to the appearance of the first signifier of relation: a rational signifier. The signifier of response to the desire for food is a starting point for the introduction of an invitatory call to relation, a starting point for constituting the relation as language—and, consequently, also for constituting thought.

4.2   Only in human beings does the primordial instinctive need for food "pass over" organically to a code of signifiers (or is an entry into it), for only in human beings is the manifestly core desire for life-as-relation mediated by a primordial instinctive need.

4.2.1   *Manifestly core* means that the desire is superior to the demand stimulated by bodily and psychological arousal. The desire has precedence over primordial instinctive need and rules over it. Hence, "un nourrisson anorexique *se fait* mourir, sa psyché est plus forte que sa régulation biologique."[2]

4.2.2   The need for food functions as a desire for life-as-relation. The desire for life-as-relation is not fully satisfied by the ingestion of food—indeed, it is never fully satisfied, and there is no way in which it can be fully satisfied. The signifier of response to the desire continues to signify (consecutively) the possibility of relation; it functions (consecutively) as invitation-to-relation, as an unbounded, never exhausted vital power for humankind.

4.2.3   The erotic (of universal relation, of intercourse) character of the desire for life defines the otherness of the mode of human existence: the rational referentiality which distinguishes a human being from every other existent thing that has life. We can rationally signify rational referentiality as the *ecstasy* (from the Greek *ek-stasis*, "standing out") of existence from any physical need on the level of vital referentiality. *Ecstasy* in this perspective means the "movement" implied by the transposition of the instinctive *need* for self-preservation into the *demand* of the desire for life-as-relation. *Movement* here has the sense of a response to the *signifier* that manifests, or refers to, a possible universal relation, a "being-with" (*syn-ousia*).

4.3   *The (rational) subject is born in the place of the Other; the subject is born when in the place of the Other, the signifier is manifested; the unconscious is constructed as language*.[3] Does the assumption and reception of these Lacanian formulations by philosophical anthropology oblige us to accept a naturalistic version and interpretation of human rationality, of human existence as *personal*?

4.3.1   The mode by which human rational existence "is born," or emerges on the horizon of our capacities for confirmation, admits rather of a naturalistic approach—an approach based on scientific observation, systematic analysis of the results of observation, and methodical checking of the analysis. Lacan demonstrated (in a coherent, scientific way) that this mode is the referentiality of desire given originally to humanity, that it is the expression of need as a demand for relation, for life-as-relation. He also showed that the rationality of human existence is precisely the power to express need as desire for relation, the making specific of desire's demand as a signifier of relation, the realization of relation through the signifiers of the demand.

4.3.2   These proofs offered by scientific psychology (like the corresponding proofs of neurophysiology, biochemistry, and other theoretical disciplines), do not exhaust the phenomenon of intellection, rationality, psychological facts, consciousness—they do not answer our anthropological questions.[4] They identify in a descriptive manner the mode of the origin of the rational subject and the biological presuppositions of this mode, but they do not account for its cause. They do not aspire to trace their way back to the definition and interpretation of the existential fact in itself, or of subjectivity as a hypostatic factor in the primordial reference, or consequently of the capacity for reasoning, of the leap of relation.

4.3.3   A hermeneutic proposition of the subject as existential fact—that is, as a fact of active existential otherness—cannot be drawn from the sciences; the role, aim, and methods of scientific knowledge are quite different. Such a proposition can only be drawn from ontological theories, which are more or less consistent with logic and with the language of our experience.

Libido and Sexuality

5 Let us repeat the obvious: it is not possible for a proposition giving an *ontological* interpretation of the human subject to be derived from *scientific* findings, for the aims and the methods of scientific knowledge are quite different from those of ontological knowledge. However, neither is it possible to construct a proposition giving an ontological interpretation without taking scientific findings into account. It is not possible for an ontological proposition to be derived from what is given, irrespective of scientific findings.

5.1   Without a "horizon" of ontological interpretation, scientific findings constitute an incomplete or deficient knowledge of reality. Without the validation conferred by a starting point that is rooted in scientific findings, the propositions of an ontological interpretation constitute arbitrary conceptualizations of reality.

5.2   If the generic difference that distinguishes humanity from every other animal is *rationality*, and if rationality is connected with the *erotic* referentiality that human desire possesses,[1] then a semantic presupposition for the construction of an ontological interpretation of the human subject is that which has been established scientifically with regard to the difference between human sexuality and the sexuality of every other animal.

5.3   In speaking generally about *sexuality*, we refer to a specific instinctive urge, a given need, an imperative for animal nature.

The need prescribes the *behavior* characteristic of the species.

The need presupposes an *object*, an individual of the opposite sex, toward which the urge is addressed.

The need has a *goal* toward which the urge is directed, which is the union of the generative organs of two individuals of different sexes (*coition*).[2]

5.3.1   We locate the sexual urge in the arousal or activation of specific organs or zones of the body (we call them *erogenous zones*) that produce pleasure.

The pleasure produced is reducible neither to the more remote goal of the urge—namely, reproduction—nor to fulfilling any other functional physiological need.

There are many different kinds of pleasurable arousal. They have various organic points of departure and lead progressively to a synthesis—that is, they are integrated to a greater or lesser extent—and they result in the climactic satisfaction of a specific organ,[3] as well as a generalized sense of psychosomatic fulfillment.

5.3.2   The *object*, an individual of the opposite sex toward which the urge is addressed, is a means or an occasion for attaining the goal of the urge. Not linked from the outset with the drive, the object of the drive is its supremely variable factor, a chance means of the procurement of pleasure.[4] From a generalized biological perspective (one which applies to all mammals), an individual of the opposite sex becomes an object of the sex drive to the degree which the individual is offered for the attainment of pleasure.

5.3.3   In what way does the behavior of the human species differ from the above generalized biological perspective?

In humans (and humans alone), sexuality is embodied in *desire*[5]—in the primordial desire for life-as-relation. That the sex drive serves the vital desire for relation—that on the level of the primordial process, the desire for life-in-itself clothes itself in the sex drive[6]—belongs to the particularity of being human.

5.3.4   The same is true of the instinct for self-preservation: it serves the desire for life-as-relation. In the primordial process of self-preservation, the desired object is not food but the breast, the touch of the mother's body, the sense of the mother's presence.[7]

5.3.5   For human beings, the object of the sex drive is that individual of the opposite sex who attracts them precisely as a possibility of functioning in terms of life-as-relation. The desire has as its object a potential second term of the longed-for relation.

5.3.6   The human drives of sexuality and self-preservation appear "in the process of psychic reality"[8] as manifestly *partial* expressions of the desire for vital relationship. The desire transcends the goal of the drives—that is, the desire is not exhausted in the satisfaction of the drives—and for that reason the desire also "embodies" the drives by highlighting their deficiency.[9]

5.3.7   The more universal given is the desire for life-as-relation. This desire clothes itself (without being exhausted) in the partial biological drives. For that reason the drives, too, can arrive at their satisfaction without remedying the deficiency. "In possessing its object, the drive learns that it is not precisely by that that it is satisfied."[10]

5.3.8   If the above statements are true, pleasure for human beings does not differ biologically from the pleasure of animals. Both cases concern the biological result that comes from the satisfaction of the drive. We use the synonyms of pleasure (enjoyment, gratification, contentment, well-being, happiness) to define noetically the generalized psychosomatic feeling that accompanies the satisfaction of biological needs, instincts, or urges. Against these we set expressions such as displeasure, annoyance, vexation, and deprivation in order to signify the opposite of pleasure.

5.4   The difference between *desire* and *drive* (on the basis of the preceding definitions) is the difference that distinguishes human beings from every other form of life.

The Ideological Basis of Naturalism

6 A coherent naturalistic version of sexuality could be summarized in the following propositions:

6.1   Human sexuality is an evolved form of the sexual (on the basis of the difference between the sexes) mode of reproduction.

In the course of its evolution, the sexual mode of reproduction manifests advantages over asexual reproduction; the sexual mode of reproduction has a clear evolutionary intentionality.

The advantage for the evolution of the species of the sexual mode of reproduction is that it introduces greater genetic variety into the population of each discrete species.

Greater genetic variety means that new combinations of transmitted genes are constantly being produced; the new combinations endow the genomes with resistance. Sexually reproduced organisms are thus able to free themselves of damaging inherited mutations more quickly than organisms that reproduce asexually.

From a long-term evolutionary perspective, the sexual mode of reproduction is accompanied by increased powers of the species to adapt to the environment, which is constantly changing in unpredictable ways.

6.2   Sexual reproduction is governed by evolutionary laws.

The female individual of each species is programmed to choose sexual partners that will serve her evolutionary interests.

The female individual secures evolutionary advantages (such as the chance of a high survival rate among her young) if she carefully chooses and mates with males who have the greatest power of producing semen, the greatest frequency of ejaculation, the greatest readiness to fulfill a parental role in the care of the young.

6.2.1   Correspondingly, the male individual is programmed to pursue a mating strategy that is most advantageous for the evolution of the species.

The male individual acquires an evolutionary advantage (from the point of view of fertilizing as many females as possible) if he is able to drive off or destroy male rivals, attract and arouse female individuals, and maintain both a constant desire for coition and a strong capacity for ensuring he has a multiplicity of mates.

6.2.2   On the basis of the evolutionary laws inherent in nature, the sexes develop capacities peculiar to each that serve the dynamics of evolution—males, for example, develop multicolored feathers, or large strong horns, tusks, or crests. Females, likewise, develop inventive strategies both for resisting the approaches of undesirable would-be mates and for attracting and arousing desirable mates.

A characteristic aspect of the law of evolution that governs sexual reproduction is the fact that in certain species (e.g., mice and men), individuals of the opposite sex are attracted selectively and mate with each other on the basis of odors secreted by their bodies. Through these bodily odors, they instinctively discriminate between potential mates and prefer different genes from their own type. In this way they choose the "good" genes—that is, the genes that are most advantageous in evolutionary terms.

6.3   This hermeneutic perspective, applied to the case of the human species, seems to subordinate every characteristic element of human erotic behavior to the intentionality of evolution. According to this view, the sense of beauty, the epistemic dynamic and richness of experience that beauty generates, the formation of criteria to delineate the beautiful and the nonbeautiful, the experience and surprise of otherness, the desire to share a life together and to dwell mutually in each other, and so forth, would have to be interpreted either as products of an evolutionary dynamic inherent in nature or as sublimated manifestations of this dynamic. The same would be true of the arts, of the rich variety of forms of dress, and of the symbolic rites of social behavior. In short, that which we call human culture would have to be attributed causally to specific biological—chiefly hormonal—stimuli of the law of reproduction.

6.4   The ideology of naturalism does not hesitate to attribute the very origin, the causal principle, of human intelligence to the evolutionary dynamic of the law of sexual reproduction:

Biologically determined sexual behavior—as well as the need for *semantic* communication that sexual behavior creates in order to attract partners of the opposite sex—must have led, through a long evolutionary process, to the formation of phenotypical characteristics (products of interaction among a wide variety of genes) transmitted by inheritance, which gave rise to the encephalic-psychological (and consequently social) particularities of human beings.

With the contribution of environmental conditions and the need for group coexistence, these phenotypical characteristics guided the evolutionary formation of neurons and neuronal circuits, with the chief aim of selecting advantages for the evolution of sexual partners.

Naturalist theory assumes that the choice of a sexual partner must be classed among the more complex decisions that an animal makes, since this theory demands not only the correlation but also the assessment of a broad spectrum of information and bears critical consequences for evolutionary adaptation.

6.5   Within the same hermeneutic perspective, the evolutionary dynamic of reproductive intentionality determines and interprets most of the elements that distinguish the human species from other species.

On account of specific evolutionary adaptations that were made in the early history of the human species (such as a bipedal posture, the enlarged dimensions of the cranium, etc.), human infants are born in an immature state in comparison with those of the species most closely related to them, the anthropoid apes. For this reason, newborn human young require a long and intensive period of parental care. On her own, the mother has difficulty meeting the demands of caring for her children; the evolutionary interests of the species require the participation of the father, too, in the protection of his offspring by assuming greater responsibility for caring for his mate and their children. Thus the so-called nuclear family is formed, an arrangement that renders the sexual relations of the couple more frequent and favors the development of the more refined demands of companionship.

6.5.1   The woman remains more selective than the man, and her choices are firmer. Her effort to ensure the greatest degree of parental care on the part of the man is expressed instinctively through demands for the permanence and exclusiveness of the relationship, with the tendency for her to acquire property rights over the man, to dominate and possess him.

In spite of all this, only with difficulty is the man rendered monogamous, for reasons that can be traced to the evolutionary prescriptions of human sexuality: by coupling with multiple partners, the male achieves an increased genetic variety in his offspring, and the basic evolutionary intentionality of sexuality is the augmentation of genetic variety.

6.6   A consistent naturalistic evolutionism maintains that the given, or instinctive, operations of the evolutionary intentionalities of human sexuality are located *before* any occurrence of "sublimation," to use Freud's term. Freud defined *sublimation* as the process that generates and shapes human activities that are phenomenologically unrelated to sexuality, the deepest motivations of which, however, flow from the power of the sex drive.

As examples of sublimation, Freud described chiefly artistic activity, intellectual research, and religiosity. The sex drive is regarded as sublimated when it is diverted to nonsexual goals that aim at socially valued objects, such as art, research, and religion.

6.6.1   Even a person's attraction has nothing to do with his or her uniqueness. By the criteria of naturalism, persons of the opposite sex are attracted to each other by a potential partner's face, since the face constitutes a fairly reliable indicator of age and reflects the potential partner's health and adaptability, and consequently whether the prospects are favorable for successful reproduction. Similarly, the physical attributes of mainly sexual attraction (the breasts, thighs, and buttocks of a woman; and the height, strength, and power of a man) function as persuasive indicators of state of nourishment and therefore of reproductive capacity, including the potential for pleasurable intercourse, successful conception, and an adequate flow of milk.

Erotic feelings and experiences, which we call love, tenderness, and practical care, are products of evolutionary self-interest; they support evolutionary adaptations and reproductive success.[1]

The Erotic Derivation of Rationality

7 Proponents of the naturalist version of human sexuality claim that it is based on *pragmatic* statements. The question is whether the *pragmatic* statements exhaust the *definition*, or the sufficient marking, of human sexuality.

7.1   The statements of the naturalistic version are *pragmatic* to the extent that they are supported by valid scientific evidence, which has been subjected to empirical verification. The way human sexuality functions, however, also includes experiences, potential but commonly accessible, that cannot be made objects of scientific investigation—experiences related to sexuality's qualities and degrees of qualities.

7.1.1   If we include within the terms of the way human sexuality functions the experiences of its qualities and degrees of qualities, then objective scientific analyses cannot designate the naturalistic explanation as the *definitive* or complete interpretation. Such analyses constitute a deficient or incomplete proposition of human sexuality. They leave unexplained certain factors of sexual behavior that are commonly confirmed in the fields of the experience of qualities.

7.1.2   The following exemplify different fields in which sexuality's qualities are experienced: (1) the subjective perception of beauty, (2) the experience of distinguishing the beautiful from the nonbeautiful, (3) the degree of desire and the degrees of plea-sure, (4) erotic reciprocity (beyond any logic), (5) erotic knowl-edge (i.e., the sudden emergence of the otherness of the other), and (6) deliberate (active) self-transcendence and self-sacrificing love.

These are examples of fields in which qualities are experienced that cannot be reduced to the objective, mechanistic logic of the naturalistic version of sexuality. The same is true of the correspond-ing fields of the experience of pain or well-being—Wittgenstein's statement makes the point well: "I cannot show my toothache to anybody else, nor can I *prove* that I have toothache."[1]

7.1.3   There is a possibility here of a double-edged "error" (in Greek, *planē,* the loss of a sense of reality, the loss of the possibility of locating reality). It would be an error to transform the scien-tific supports of the naturalistic version of sexuality into *ideologi-cal* principles capable of interpreting even the fields of qualitative experience that are not reducible to objective facts (a *materialist ideology*). It would likewise be an error to transform that which in the field of qualitative experience is not reducible to objective facts into ideological principles, with a view to arriving at a unified holis-tic version of scientific interpretation and subjective experience (an *idealistic ideology*).

7.1.4   We call an *ideology* any theoretical construction deliber-ately framed to support *a priori* convictions. Again, "both the athe-ist, who scorns religion because he has found no *evidence* for its tenets, and the believer, who attempts to *prove* the existence of God, have fallen victim to the 'other'—to the idol-worship of the scientific style of thinking."[2]

7.1.5   The reception, interpretation, or knowledge of reality pre-supposes both unbiased research and respect for the limitations and capabilities of the scientific method. The common human ex-perience of qualities belongs to our knowledge of reality but is not susceptible to investigation by the scientific method. It constitutes an epistemic fact subject to common experience but not subject-able to the common language—not subjectable to assertions signi-fied by an objectified code of understanding.

7.2   The naturalist version of reality asserts that in human sexuality there are real manifestations of evolutionary determinism—manifestations, that is, of inflexible biological intentionalities that govern human nature. But the use of these assertions alone does not explain the *totality*, the whole fact, of human sexuality or its multiformity, which is not reducible to basic elements. What chiefly remains unexplained is the *existential* leap (i.e., a leap relating to the mode of existence), which we attribute specifically to human beings, with sexuality as its radically fundamental key point. This is a leap from urge to desire, from desire to language, from language to the many-faceted nature (the "infinity of parts"[3]) of epistemic potentiality, from a predetermined capacity to perform certain skills to a *creative* otherness; a leap, finally, from the undifferentiated individual of a natural uniform species to the subject of self-conscious, active (not merely morphic) otherness—that is to say, a leap to the subject of freedom from what is predetermined by nature.

7.2.1   The key point at which the fundamental *rational* referentiality of the human subject is constituted is sexuality. Already on the level of libido, natural determinacy is interwoven with the objective of—or the desire for—*life-as-relation*: life as freedom from nature. "It is in any case in desire that the essential element of the primordial process is determined."[4] The "specifically human" is initially located in the possibility for libido to be expressed as a desire and demand for relation. Although the birth of the biological individual is subject to what is prescribed by nature, the birth of the rational subject is the fruit of desire; it is a work of relation. The already existing brain is not the starting point for the constitution of the rational subject; the brain activates the desire for life-as-relation, or realizes this existential demand, which is the foundation of human particularity. The *relation constitutes reason, not reason the relation*. What we call the human subject is an erotic fact, and because it is an erotic fact, it is also a rational being.

7.2.2   With regard to the reproductive-evolutionary law that governs sexuality, the potentiality for relation creates a discontinuity, a discontinuity in a given existential reality that, once the split has occurred, cannot be abolished.

7.2.3   The partial—relative but always real—freedom from nature (the existential leap of relation) does not overturn the laws of nature; it presupposes them in order to transcend them. The relation is activated by the energies or powers of nature. And at the same time, *relation* transcends as a fact the predetermined necessities that govern the natural operations.

7.2.4   What does it mean that relation *transcends* nature? It means that relation is differentiated existentially from nature, that it constitutes a different mode of existence. The existential mode of the relation—even though it is activated by the energies, or powers, of nature—contains potentialities for freedom from the predeterminations, or necessities, of nature.

The potentialities for freedom from the operation of the law of nature are received by us as something advantageous and excellent. That is why we say that the relation *transcends* nature.

7.2.5   The *mode* by which we attain or, more accurately, approach freedom from nature is not alien to the way we function naturally. The existential leap from nature (determinacy) to meta-nature (freedom) presupposes nature and at the same time transcends it.

7.2.6   Nature (determinacy) and meta-nature (relation) are intertwined with human sexuality from the beginning, as a protean process, just as they are also intertwined in the functioning of the conscious and the unconscious.

7.2.7   Linguistic signifiers manifesting freedom from nature—manifesting life-as-relation—are *selflessness*, *self-transcendence*, *self-denial*, *love*, and *erotic yearning*.

7.3   In human beings (and only in human beings), the need for food, the urge for self-preservation, serves the desire for life-as-relation—a desire that renders a human being a rational subject. The desire for life-as-relation has precedence; it belongs to the protean process. And it is mediated by the need for food.

Moreover, in human beings (and only in human beings) sexual need, the urge to perpetuate life, functions as libido. It serves the desire for life-as-relation, the desire for unlimited life in every unfulfilled fullness of relation, which renders a human being a rational subject.

7.3.1   Even before Lacan advanced his analyses, the Freudian version already interpreted libido as synonymous with love, and hunger as synonymous with the instinct for nourishment.[5]

Libido, according to Freud, is in opposition to the urge for self-preservation.[6]

Libido conserves its sexual character while at the same time it "remains an expression of the drives which are related to whatever we can conceive of as love."[7]

In his book *Jenseits des Lustprinzips* (1920), Freud introduces the concept of *erotic love* as the fundamental principle of our basic drives, as a term synonymous with the drive for life and opposite to the drive for death,[8] often identifying erotic love with libido.[9]

7.3.2   The human infant begins life without reason, thought, judgment, or imagination. It is born endowed only with the desire for life-as-relation, which has come to be signified by the Latin word *libido* (desire, yearning).

Desire for life-as-relation is mediated initially by the desire for the mother's breast, the mother's body, the mother's presence—her embrace, her tenderness, and her affection.

This desire is mediated progressively by every call to relationship, which creates in the recipient of the call the desire for a permanent and complete union (i.e., intercourse, or *syn-ousia*, which in Greek has the root meaning of "being with") with the invitatory fact. The invitatory fact, the occasion or stimulus of the desire for *syn-ousia*, has for the recipient of the call the dynamic of beauty—which is precisely the dynamic of invitation. The beauty can be that of the human person, but it can also be an indirect manifestation of the person: a gesture, a smile, the grace of the body, a song, a musical composition, a painting, a poem. A fact invitatory to *syn-ousia* can also be something beautiful in the natural world: a sunset, the sea, a flower, a landscape.

At some point in the growth of biological maturity and after, the desire for life-as-relation is also mediated by sexual need. Just like the vital need for food, the vital sexual need makes the desire for life-as-relation specific in existential activities, without ever exhausting the desire.

7.3.3   The *logos*, or rational principle, of beauty is that which is able to signify the potentiality for the fulfillment of the—in any event—unfulfillable vital desire. We also reckon within the field of the invitatory power an objective readiness for unpremeditated non-self-interested relation, for self-transcendence and self-offering: the uninterpreted gift of reciprocity. At the same time, a vital factor of *beauty* is the revelatory dynamic of otherness—the unique, dissimilar, and unrepeatable aspect of the invitatory fact as an immediacy of experiential affirmation.

7.3.4   Beauty is an invitatory *logos*, or principle, calling us to a vital relation, and this *logos* is signified by the language of art, of religion—of culture as a whole. All language of this kind belongs to the field of the experience of qualities. Their interpretation as "sublimated" manifestations of the reproductive dynamic belonging to evolution is a hypothetical proposition of mechanistic logic with obvious and enormous hermeneutic gaps.

Brain, Consciousness, Subject

8 Relation as existential fact, a fact definitive of the mode of existence, is made operative by the energies, or powers, of nature, while it also "contains" the possibilities of freedom from natural law.

As a result of what natural operations is relation achieved? What are the natural (biological) preconditions for the realization of relation and therefore of freedom from the predeterminations (necessities) of nature?

8.1 We can identify some kind of relation in certain species of irrational animal, relations that they create with other animals or with human beings. Projecting our human experience, we speak of animals' *relations* of maternal and paternal care for their young, of *relations* of trust and gratitude toward whoever provides them with food and protection.

8.1.1 The biological basis for such relations is clearly the brain function of memory in conjunction with the reflexive instinct of self-preservation. The (always pleasurable) response to the need for food and protection must be connected in the animal's memory with the provider of this pleasure—with the visual, olfactory, or other assurances of his or her presence. Thus what we call the *faithfulness*, *gratitude*, or *friendship* of the animal functions more in accordance with the character of Pavlovian reflexes.

8.2   In the field of our human experience, that which we call *relation* is a fact that presupposes (1) self-knowledge of the *I*, (2) consciousness of the otherness of the *you* or the *it*, (3) the intellectual (critical) categorization of the difference, and (4) the linguistic power to communicate, or signify, both the experience of self-knowledge and otherness, and the intellectual (critical) categorization of the experience.

8.2.1   Memory (the retrospective sense) of pleasure or displeasure, security or threat, does not signify the functioning of consciousness and therefore cannot be the foundation of the fact of relation. Consciousness is presupposed by the knowledge of the uniqueness of the sensation and the otherness of its cause. At least, that is how human experience is described.

Without memory, consciousness cannot exist. But memory alone does not manifest consciousness. Memory is a necessary but also an insufficient condition for the existence of consciousness.

8.3   In the field of human experience, relation is a conscious fact—consciousness constitutes a necessary condition for the realization of relation.

Is consciousness the biological, or natural, precondition of relation? We know that brain damage can occur that inhibits or prevents the functioning of consciousness. Can we infer from this that consciousness is a natural, biological given, that it is a result of a process on an absolutely material level—on the level of the brain?

8.3.1   Such an inference cannot be controlled scientifically so as to acquire scientific validation.

A presupposition of scientific validity is the possibility of *objective* assertions, assertions that are susceptible to common verification—that is, they may be verified by anybody—either by direct observation or by observation under laboratory conditions (i.e., by experimental control).

The phenomenon of consciousness cannot be subjected to the terms of *objective*, scientific control, for it can be confirmed only as subjective experience, an experience of absolute subjective otherness. Moreover, as an empirical given of subjective otherness, consciousness precedes and defines the *mode*, or process, and the very

possibility of any assertion, as well as the mode and the very possibility of any attempt at confirming assertions.

It does not belong to my natural powers to ascertain (to observe
and objectify) the mode, or process, by which the other becomes
conscious of phenomena, or to ascertain the ability of the other
to become conscious of them. I am unable to know, for example,
whether that which any particular other becomes conscious of as
a red color is the same as that which I myself become conscious of
as red.

8.3.2   Consciousness is a *necessary* presupposition for the realization of relation, and the brain is a *necessary* presupposition for
the functioning of consciousness. Is consciousness also a *sufficient*
condition for the realization of relation? Is the brain also a *sufficient* condition for the functioning of consciousness? Finally, is the
brain the biological, or natural, precondition for relation?

8.3.3   An affirmative reply with valid scientific support cannot be
given to these questions. The study of the human brain seems to
come up against certain boundaries beyond which scientific, objective assertion is unattainable. For example:

(a) Scientific research has validly "mapped out" the functions
of the brain to a large extent: experts know *what* happens *where*.
It has been established, however, that no noetic or intellectual
function is the direct result of the action of a particular area of
the brain or of the coordination of particular areas. Something
intervenes between the causal provocation of a cerebral function
and the function itself. That something which intervenes con-
cerns the behavior of the whole brain, not the behavior of parts
or sections of it.

(b) We validly assert that the human brain, in its structure and
function, has absolute individual otherness. The brain of every being (who has existed, exists, or will exist) has a structure, an organization, that is unique and unrepeatable, dissimilar to that of
every other being. With the help of scientific technology, it may be
asserted that the otherness of each brain is not only syntactical or
morphological but is also an otherness of continuous becoming.
The networks of neurons of every brain are in a state of constant

change, a change that is self-organized. The brain is an organ that is constantly organizing itself.

(c) The self-organization of the brain—the otherness of this becoming—is interwoven with subjective self-consciousness. In this interweaving, there is apparent a sequence of cause and effect that works in both directions—something analogous to the indeterminacy or duality of physical phenomena on a microscopic scale (the theory of wave-particle duality). What neurophysiologists have determined permits the paradoxical linguistic statement that, just as consciousness is a "product" of the brain, so too the function of the brain is a "product" of consciousness. Although in the embryo the assemblage, or organization, of the brain comes about through instructions encoded in the genes, after birth the connections between the neurons are also determined by the functioning of consciousness, just as they are also determined by social factors—factors, that is, of the human environment.

(d) From some point in the growing maturity of the human infant and after, the assemblage, or organization, of cerebral functions—that is, the interconnections between neurons—is a result of consciousness. Indicative of this is the interweaving of consciousness with the "codification" of optical information (on different levels of the functioning of neurons); this codification is the critical abstractive reduction of sensory representations to unified mental images (*ideas*; from the Greek verb *idein*, "to see") that are impressed upon (or recorded in) the mind. These images remain in the mind (*en nōi*) and thus become *ennoies*, or "concepts."

(e) The end result of the interweaving is the "linguification" of optical stimuli and representations—that is to say, their combination with symbolic *acoustic images*, with the *signifiers* of the linguistic code. The mode by which the brain's objective functions (e.g., the processes which ensure chromatic vision) are combined with the noetic world of subjectivity, the mode by which these functions create subjective experiences, is a mode not subject to a scientific approach and justifies our postulating the two-way reciprocal influence of consciousness and the brain.[1]

(f) The self-organization of the brain as an otherness of its syntactic-morphological becoming is interwoven with subjective self-consciousness preeminently (?) in the case of the *critical* and *imaginative* functioning of the intellect. Every human being has his or her own unique and dissimilar sensory representations, chiefly visual, of objects of the same kind. From these representations, the mind subtracts the circumstantial characteristics peculiar to the individual object and forms a single fixed image: an idea, or concept. The image summarizes those necessary characteristics that are sufficient to define the homogeneity of the species, the characteristics which enable every partial object—in Greek, *antikeimenon*, that which "lies opposite"—to be manifested by the common name of the specific homogeneity of the species. At the same time, however, along with this critical subtractive function, which reduces the otherness of individual representations or experiences to common and communicable ideas or concepts, the mind also has an imaginative capacity: an ability to combine, coordinate, and organize concepts, to produce syntheses or new concepts, and so forth. The critical and imaginative function of intellection is a characteristic field in which the two-way interaction of consciousness and the brain takes place.

8.4   One of the manifestations of human intellectual behavior is what we call intuition: *intuitus intellectualis*—a great problem for establishing epistemic objectivity in Western philosophical thought from as early as the time of Nicholas of Cusa right up to that of Kant and Husserl or Merleau-Ponty. Intuition has been described as "the knowledge which comes from nowhere": it does not emerge from observation or from logical analysis, nor is it subject to a prescribed method. Intuition is the causeless arrival at knowledge or at a solution or choice—it emerges unexpectedly and without justification. By a leap, the mind apprehends something without being able to identify the *how* and the *why*.

8.4.1   The role of intuition is of capital importance in mathematics. Intuition constructs mathematics as a language referring to realities that are inaccessible to sensory confirmation. The role of intuition has proved to be decisive for modern scientific discoveries; it has displaced the inductive method in favor of deduction, the formation of propositions interpretative of reality on the basis of the intuitive conception of a general hermeneutic principle. The intuitive identification of the general principle takes precedence and is validated by the verification of the propositions which are deduced from it.[2]

8.4.2   Is intuition a function of the brain, or should it be attributed to the indeterminacy of consciousness?

This question identifies yet another point in the interpretation of human rationality beyond which scientific, objective certainty is unattainable.

As with consciousness itself, we have no scientific support for attributing intuition to some other factor outside the brain. But neither do we have any scientific support for attributing intuition (again, as with consciousness itself) to brain function alone.

Between the natural (chemical, electrical, biological) processes of the brain and consciousness or intuition there is an unbridgeable hermeneutic gap: the transformation of the external stimuli received by the brain into the experience of consciousness—into an experience of subjective self-knowledge, into the knowledge of the otherness of every subjective experience—remains scientifically indeterminable and inexplicable.

(Frequently in mathematics or in systematic scientific research, intuition favors choices and solutions that logic rejects. In such circumstances the methodological reversal of the direction of the research—from the result of the choice of a solution to the initial intuitive idea—can lead to an *a posteriori* verification of the originally nonrational intuition.)

8.4.3   Brain damage or the aging of the brain can destroy intuition or even consciousness. They can change or destroy even the function of language. Thus we return to the following question: given that the brain is a *necessary* condition, is it also *sufficient* for the existence of consciousness, intuition, and language?

The symbolic-referential function of language frequently presupposes an intuitive apprehension of what is expressed, especially when one is dealing with the *sense* of a sentence, with the semantics of syntax (the syntactical assembly and structure of a sentence). At the same time, the intuitive apprehension of linguistic symbolics—

the attribution of meaning to reality through the subjective transition from linguistic signifiers to experiential signifieds—presupposes the functioning of self-consciousness, that is, of conscious self-knowledge.

Consciousness, language, and intuition are clearly interwoven with each other, in conditions of indeterminacy, constituting a single, unified state of active becoming. If one were to add to this assertion the organic interweaving of language and thought, thought and judgment, judgment and imagination, imagination and memory, then (in conditions of indeterminacy) the unified state of active becoming broadens out to include the totality of the properties of the *rational* subject.

8.4.4   The unified state of active becoming of subjective rationality is clearly an articulation (with real terms, in conditions of indeterminacy) of the functions of the brain. But it is equally an articulation of the *environment*, both physical and social, of every human being.

This second assertion is supported by converging aphoristic inferences that together form the commonplaces of neurobiology and clinical psychology, from a frequently disparate hermeneutic perspective. Some characteristic examples of such aphorisms follow.

(a) The self-conscious ego is socially constructed. The conscious ego of every human being is created through social interaction (Gerald Edelman).

(b) The brain and the nervous system cannot be explained independently of physical conditions and social interactions. These conditions, however, both environmental and social, are undetermined and open (Hilary Putnam).

(c) Understanding emerges as a result of interactions on many different levels of organization, ranging from the molecular to the social (Gerald Edelman).

(d) The semiological content of understanding necessarily presupposes its referential function: the possibility of reference to objects, to states, to participants in the experience of objects and states (John Searle).

(e) Every individual understanding creates its own version of reality through social and linguistic mutual influences (Hilary Putnam).

(f) A computer cannot (nor will it ever be able to) give *meaning* to the symbols on which it works, precisely because it is unable to accord them *referentiality*, to recognize a cross-reference in them (Roger Penrose).

(g) We must abandon the idea of a genetically programmed mechanism for acquiring language (Gerald Edelman).

(h) Language is generated through social interaction in the course of events that bring about the beginning of the formation of links between *meanings* and *phonemes* (Steven Pinker, Mark Johnson).

(i) The connection of sensory stimuli with the subjectivity (uniqueness) of experiences does not admit of any *a priori* comprehensive description in terms of effective processes. The only thing that we can say is that this connection is not unrelated to the insertion of the subject into the language of a community (John Searle).

(j) If the subject is defined by language and reason, this means that the subject *in initio* is constituted in the space of the Other—the subject is generated so long as the signifier is manifested in the field of the Other (Jacques Lacan).[3]

8.4.5 To dwell for a moment on this point, the unified state of active becoming of subjective rationality is clearly an articulation (with real limitations, in conditions of indeterminacy) of functions of the brain. But it is equally also an articulation of the physical and social *environment* of every human being, the articulation of the relations of every human being with nature and society.

Nature and *relations* (with nature and with one's fellow human beings) constitute the necessary and sufficient conditions for the rationality of the human subject. Nature (in this case, the brain and the nervous system) is the *means*, or *instrument*, and relation is the *mode*, or the *how*, of subjective rationality.

The findings of neurobiology and clinical psychology up to the present day appear to converge in establishing that the means, or instrument, of subjective rationality (nature) serves the mode, or the how, of subjective rationality (relation) without wholly determining it. The brain and the nervous system influence and define the possibilities of relation, but they also leave real margins for the indeterminacy (freedom) of relation.

Relation is activated through nature without being bound *definitively* by nature. Moreover, nature is activated (is realized existentially) as relation, yet it is *also* defined by relation: the brain and the nervous system are formed not only by genetic instructions but also by environmental influences.

The margins for the indeterminacy of relation—for freedom from the predeterminations or necessities of nature—and the margins for the causal definition of nature by relation (always with real limitations of the existential fact) set the boundaries of the logical space of meaning: of the *ontology of relation*.

Again the Semiology of Relation

9 The active becoming of human rationality is an articulation of brain functions and environmental influences (from both the physical and social environments); it is an articulation of the relations of every human being with nature and with society (i.e., the organized collectivity of our fellow human beings).

9.1   Our relation with nature includes, for example, the following:

(a) the reception and bodily assimilation of nature "lying opposite" us through breathing and taking in food and drink;

(b) the reception of nature "lying opposite" us as sensory impression and experience (through sight, hearing, touch, taste, and smell), with a corresponding psychological reception of impressions and experiences (satisfaction, dissatisfaction, delight, displeasure, gladness, annoyance, enjoyment, anxiety, pleasure, pain, etc.) and also a processing of sensory impressions by the intellect, the memory, the imagination, and the critical faculty;

(c) the reception and transformation of nature "lying opposite" us into tools, clothing, improved powers of ensuring food (the cultivation of the land, the raising of livestock, the development of manufacturing skills, etc.); and

(d) the reception and transformation of nature (colors, stone, wood, metal, sounds, etc.) into a *logos*, or language, of art, a language that is able to signify emotions, social experience, interpretation of reality; the transformation of colors into a language of painting; of sounds into a language of music; of stone, metal, clay, and wood into sculpture and also into the language of architecture, town planning, and so forth.

9.2   Our relation with our fellow human beings—human collectivity and society—comprises, for example:

(a) the consequences that, in the very first stage of human life, the bodily contact of the infant with its mother's body has for the self-awareness of the boundaries of individuality;

(b) the consequences that, in the same first stage of life, flow from the referential location of the infant's libido in the mother's breast, her embrace, her presence;

(c) the consequences that the appearance of the first signifier in the place of the Other—that is, the progressive insertion of the referentiality of desire into the given linguistic code of the society in which the infant is born—has for the generation of the rational subject;

(d) the effects that flow from the appearance (on the horizon of the infant's awareness) of the father as a barrier or boundary marker to the (Oedipal) desire for relation with the mother and the socialization of desire (and of referentiality) that follows; and

(e) the consequences that the specific social environment in which the human subject is set (comprising educational, political, and cultural institutions, the cultivation of the mind, historical conditioning, manners, customs, etc.) has in the formation of subjective rationality and its otherness—that is, in the formation of a linguistic instrument and mode of thought; the development of intellectual capacities; the cultivation of expressive possibilities, epistemic sensitivity, perspicacity, intuition, and so forth.

9.3   Let us dwell on the semiological distinctions. By the term *relation* (*schesis*) we mean generally the linking or mutual dependence of two natural givens, the connection and articulation between the two (or between them and other givens). In this sense, we also use the word *relation* for the mutual interaction between living organisms and their physical environment and for the vital or existential dependence of every animate being (and consequently of humanity) on inanimate nature.

9.3.1   By the same term, *relation*, however, we also identify the exclusively human, and wholly peculiar to humanity, idea of *goal setting* (*stochothesia*) with respect to the primordial life-giving desire—the life-giving *goal* (*stochos*) of the primordial appetitive referentiality. *Relation* indicates a given goal setting, and consequently a definitive *mode of existence* (*tropos tēs hyparxeōs*).

By the word *relation* we identify the fact that only in humankind does appetitive referentiality encounter in the place of its reference (the space of the Other) a *mark* of the power to respond to the desire. This mark, or *signifier,* of the power to respond is the dynamic starting point—and, moreover, the potential recapitulation in contrast to every other animate being—of a peculiar mode of referential reciprocity: a mode by which the reference acts and is received as language and intellection constituting self-awareness and consciousness.

By the term *relation* we define and delineate the generation and realization of the rational subject in the space of the Other.

9.3.2   By the term *relation* we define and delineate, then, a real fact—that is, one verified by common experience—a fact brought into being within the terms of the law of nature, but with a result not subject to our hermeneutic understanding of the law of nature. The newly born offspring of every mammal has a desire for food *through* the relation with its mother, but only the human neonate has a desire for food *as* relation. This distinction between the goals of the desire—inexplicable simply in terms of the law of nature— constitutes a leap of existential difference: a transition (*metastasis*) to another mode of existence.

The Causal Mode of Freedom

10 After our many digressions exploring the different senses of the word *relation*, we return to the point raised in paragraph 3.5.3, the question of the *absolute existential freedom of God*, thanks to which alone the *relative freedom of humanity* can have logical space—in order that existential freedom should provide an etiological clarification of rational human subjectivity.

10.1   With the definition "God is love,"[1] Christian experience proposes an ontological hermeneutic that in the signifier *love* (*agapē*) summarizes absolute existential freedom (i.e., the *being* of God). In the language of the religious traditions and the philosophical systems as a rule, the signifier *God* refers to an existence free from limitations of beginning, end, space, time, change, mutation, decay, and death. Christian ecclesial experience, however, had historically to confront the very specific challenge that it had inherited from ancient Greek philosophical thought: whether we can identify an *a priori* possibility of existential freedom— whether the causal principle of the existential fact is freedom or necessity.

10.1.1   In the experience of the ancient Greeks, it is only by intellection (*to noein*) that we can identify being (*to einai*). For that reason alone, humanity endowed with mind can confirm that which exists as existent and can identify, as well, the *mode* of this existence.

The *mind* is the *place* of the knowledge of being (*to einai*) and of beings (*tōn ontōn*), of the modes and forms of being (*the place of forms . . . the perception of sensible things is the mind*).[2] And this is because all existent things exist *according to their participation in that which is intelligible*,[3] which means that they exist in the degree to which they participate in a prehypothetical intelligible reality defining the mode-form-*logos* of their existence.

A universal (*xynos*) *logos*-mind preexists with respect to existent things, a given rationality with an unexplained cause, *a most divine and dispassionate energy*, which *exists in* or is *brought into being in* existent things as their *essence* (the specific *mode* of their existence),[4] *like art is to its material* and *like light makes potential colors into actual colors.*[5] Thus *when one says mind,* one is referring to *the cause of the world and all its order.*[6]

10.1.2   If God exists, then he is himself existentially bound to the intelligible *logos* that is definitive of his existence, to the *logos* of his *essence*. Even God is that which his essence defines him to be: he cannot be something other than what he is as God.

10.1.3   The Greek word for *essence* (*ousia*) is a derivative of the feminine form of the present participle of the verb *to be* (*einai*): the essence manifests the mode of participation in being, the mode that makes every existent thing what it *is* (a human being, a horse, a lily, etc.). In the word *mode* (*tropos*), we summarize those characteristics (the given logoi) that make *every* human being a human being, *every* horse a horse, *every* lily a lily, and God God.

10.1.4   In the ancient Greek perspective, the mode by which the human mind conceives of God and the attributes which it accords to him correspond to the reality of God, because *being* is realized only *by intellectual participation*, only as subject to the necessity of its rational prescriptions: *everything occurs for a reason and by necessity.*[7] It is necessary for there to be *something divine . . . that which is not moved but is the mover . . . infinite, dispassionate, immutable.*[8]

10.2   The fundamental starting point of the Christian gospel is the fact of the *incarnation of God*. If this refers to a true historical fact, then ancient Greek ontology is clearly overturned: if God can also exist as a human being without ceasing to be God—if he can really *be* human and not merely *appear* to be so—then the existence of God is demonstrated to be free from logical prescriptions of essence or nature. God is then existentially free from every necessity of mode of existence and can therefore also exist by the mode of human essence or nature (as a perfect human being) without ceasing to be God.

Moreover, if the possibility exists that being (*hyparxis*) might be free from the prescriptions and necessities of essence or nature, and if the fact of this existential freedom is the causal principle of what exists, then there is a logical space for the "grace" (the gift of being) that God can bestow on humanity with a view to humanity's sharing itself in the mode of freedom from the necessities of its essence or nature—namely, the necessities of decay, of death—limitations that accompany the nature of created being.

Within the perspective of ancient Greek ontology, all these possibilities are simply *foolishness.*[9]

10.3   The fact that before the Christian Church fully took root in society, it had become part of the Greek, or Hellenized, world of the Roman Empire and expressed itself in the philosophical language of that world is quite remarkable. Even the earliest texts proclaiming the Church's message are couched in language that refutes ancient Greek rationalism: a language consistent with the semantics of the ontological theories that were to follow historically and that were to constitute a systematic hermeneutical proposition emphasizing the absolute existential freedom of God.

10.3.1 From the very start of its historical life, the Christian Church has referred to a *triadic* God, to a triad of hypostases of the Godhead (i.e., to three specific existences) that makes the divine *being* an existential reality.

Ecclesial experience has, from the very first, maintained that the divine being "is love"—not that God *has* love, or that love is a moral and qualitative characteristic of God (a property of the way he acts), nor that God first exists and because he exists, he loves. The phrase *God is love* reveals precisely that which the phrase *God is triadic* also reveals—both phrases signify the mode that makes God that which he is, the mode that makes God *be* God.

This mode is not omnipotence, omniscience, ingenerateness, or immortality. From the first texts recording the Church's experience, the mode of existence that differentiates God from every existent thing is his absolute existential freedom, a freedom from any predetermination, necessity, or rational prescription of existence. Both the signifier *love* (*agapē*)—because we understand love only as an active choice and not as a necessity—and the linguistic signifiers that refer to the triad of the hypostases of God refer to this absolute existential freedom.

10.3.2 The linguistic signifiers that ecclesial experience has used to identify the three hypostases of the Godhead reveal (1) the *personal* character of the hypostases (existences with self-consciousness and rationality); (2) the existential otherness of every hypostasis, that is, its unique, dissimilar, and unrepeatable character; and (3) the existential, or life-giving, relation that connects each hypostasis with the other two hypostases.

The signifiers, or names, of the personal hypostases of God are, in the language of the Church, *Father*, *Son*, and *Spirit*; these signifiers were in use from the first moment of the Church's historical life and a considerable time before the appearance of a systematically articulated ontology.

10.3.3 The names of the personal hypostases of the triadic Godhead reveal existence not as self-contained[10] atomicity—not as a unit of existential autonomy,[11] but as a mode and fact of *relation*, of *self-transcendence*, of *love*. The names indicate that the existence of each hypostasis of the triadic God is realized as a *relationship of love*, that each hypostasis *exists* as love, that it *is* love.

By signifying relation and the dynamic of relation, the names of the hypostases of the triadic God realize the possibility that one signifier should indicate both the subjective identity, the existential otherness, of each hypostasis and the common mode of existence of the three hypostases (i.e., love).

10.3.4 What is signified linguistically by the name *Father* is both the subjective identity (or existential otherness) of the causal principle of divine being and also a mode of existence that does not bind the hypostasis to atomic self-containedness. The name *Father* indicates that the specific hypostasis of God is neither known nor exists in itself and for itself but only as the "begetter" (*gennētōr*) of the Son and the "processor" (*ekporeuōn*) of the Spirit. The Father *hypostasizes* his *being*—that is, makes his being a hypostasis, a real existence—in a loving mode (*agapētikōs*), begetting the Son and causing the Spirit to proceed.

This *being* of the Father's is indicated not only by his divinity but also by his *fatherhood*, his uncircumscribed and non-predetermined freedom to exist because he loves, a freedom that is confirmed by the begetting of the Son and the procession of the Spirit. The name *Father* signifies this freedom not simply as a fact related to the will but as the cause of the Being's being hypostasized—that is, the cause of its constituting existential hypostases. The freedom, the causal principle of the existent, is signified linguistically as the causal principle of *being* because it is identified with the hypostatic self-determination of God as Father, that is to say, as *love*: he exists and constitutes the cause of the existence not because he is God but because he wills to be the *Father*—wills to exist as freedom of loving self-transcendence and self-offering.

10.3.5 The same absolute existential freedom is also indicated by the name *Son*; in the sonship, a hypostasis of being is signified that is not predetermined existentially by its nature or essence but that is, rather, self-determined as freedom of relation to the Father. The relation is loving, that is to say, free from causal existential dependence. The Son wills to exist because he loves the Father; his love is signified by the name *Son* as an existential response to the freedom of the love of the Father, the causal principle of existence.

The Son exists without his existence preceding his sonship, without its being bound existentially to predeterminations of ontic (atomic) self-containedness. That which he *is* is signified precisely by the *voluntary* sonship, not by the *essential* (i.e., belonging to essence and therefore necessary) divinity. He is *God* because he exists as *Son of the Father*, because his existence corresponds to and refers to the life-giving will of the Father: the

Son hypostasizes the freedom of love, its non-subordination to existential necessities.

The Son is also signified by the name *Logos* (Word) of the Father: his existence makes known the Father and the Father's will, which is creative, cosmopoeic, and salvific of creatures. The *Logos* of God *witnesses* to the Father, without his existence preceding his witness: his existential witness hypostasizes the sonship; the sonship of the Son is the Logos of the Father, the making known of the Father's will. This will of the Father's has the same logical space in the language of the Church as does the divine *being*: *love* as absolute existential freedom, as a voluntary convergence of the wills of the three hypostases of the Godhead.

A voluntary and loving convergence of the three personal wills in a common will and energy of the Godhead is signified in the language of the Church from the first moment, with the "mission" (*sending*) of the Spirit (the *Paraclete*) by the Logos. As Logos, the Son *witnesses* to the Father as *sending* the Spirit, who is the personal accomplisher of the manifestation of God "outside" God as ontopoeic and life-bearing love.[12]

10.3.6 Language is stretched, reaching the limits of its expressive possibilities in order to prove the astonishingly accurate aim of the signifiers that Christian experience has made use of. These signifiers were being used by Christians even before any shaping of a systematic ontological context had begun—used with a view to referring to hypostases of the divine *being*, of a single existential identity and common, loving mode of existence.

Personal (i.e., self-willed, self-activated, self-conscious) hypostasis should be noted not as an atomic onticity and an existential identity existing in itself but as a loving relation and referential realization—that is to say, as freedom transcending any defining autonomy.

This is exactly what the word *Spirit* seeks to convey: the active hypostatic otherness should be revealed—otherness that exists by referring "through its work" to the being of the love of the Father, to divine love as ontopoeic and life-giving truth. This is connected with the *Spirit of the Father* as the opposite number (by linguistic logic) to the *Logos of the Father*: the Logos is begotten

by the Father and witnesses by his existence to God as the Father
of love. The Spirit proceeds from the Father (the causal principle
of existential freedom), and thus the Spirit's existence indicates
the "property" of God, his identity as creative, life-giving love.[13]

The Limits of Ontological Realism

11 It seems that Christian experience, in its written testimonies and in the first centuries (at least) of its historical journey—for as long as the Greek cultural tradition remained operative in the societies of the period—was clearly aware of the relativity of language, especially when language refers to metaphysics.

11.1 Language conveys a relative—not a complete, not a precise—knowledge. There is always an epistemic gap between the *understanding* of the signifiers and the experiential *knowledge* of the things signified. This gap becomes even greater when the linguistic signifiers convey meaning without constructing images (or clusters of images) of sensible reality.

11.1.1 "The limits of my *language* mean the limits of my world."[1] They are identified with the limits of human sensory experience, with the psychological effects this experience produces, with the creative (i.e., combinatory-syntactical) products of intellection, imagination, and intuition. It is only relatively, obliquely, and figuratively (*as in a mirror dimly*[2]) that language signifies the reality of God—of God, who from the beginning has been defined by Christian experience as *inexpressible, inconceivable, invisible, incomprehensible.*[3]

11.1.2 Language refers to the existential *reality* of an inconceivable and incomprehensible God (not to mental idols: humanly

56

constructed psychological concepts, imagined self-evident truths) when it functions as a vehicle for sharing the experience of the historical data of divine-human relations.

The sharing of this experience constitutes the body of relations of communion that is the Church. And the formation of this body (the social transmission of experience) is served by language. Outside this body of relations, this experience, the language of Christian theology records metaphysical problems (as does the language of any coherent philosophical analysis). It does not function referentially, and it does not refer experientially to existential (*metaphysical*, or "beyond the physical") reality.

11.1.3   We speak of God "following the measure of our own language (for it is not possible for us to transcend our language)."[4]

11.1.4   The very concept of *existence* cannot be correlated intellectually with the sense of the word *God*: the uncreated cause of the existential fact must, according to the measure of our perceptive capacities, be something other than (i.e., different from) the existent products of this cause.

11.1.5   That is why even "existence in the proper sense cannot be attributed to God . . . Nor that [the divine] is, nor that it is comprehended; you should conceive of it thus; but that it not even *is*; for this is knowing in unknowing."[5] "And for this reason it is more appropriate to attribute nonbeing [to God] rather than transcendence of being."[6]

11.1.6   Within the limits set by the semantics of our language, the limits of our world, it makes better sense to say *God does not exist* than to say *God exists*. He does not exist in the modes by which we understand existence. All that we know, all that we can conceive of or imagine, falls short of the reality of God. "All things fall short of God, not locally (*topōi*) but by nature."[7]

11.1.7   The radical apophaticism of ecclesial experience finds its most direct expression in the so-called Areopagitical writings of the fifth century. God is neither spirit, not sonship, nor fatherhood. He is neither divinity, nor goodness, neither mind, nor reason, nor intellection, nor number, nor power, nor light, nor life, "nor anything else known by us or by any other being."⁸ All the characteristics that we can attribute to God emerge by analogy or by antithesis from the knowledge of our own human existence or of the existence of other existent things that we know through our senses and our intellect. God, however, must be defined as a given *transcending every positive statement* and *transcending every negation, beyond* whatever we can conceive of or imagine.

11.2   If we consistently follow the epistemological presuppositions of the validity of knowledge—as we know them from science and also from our experience of life—we must reject as arbitrary any possibility of *knowledge* of God and of *relation* with God. It is epistemologically completely inconsistent for us to attribute self-consciousness, reason, thought, judgment, and memory (self-evidently) to God, for these are characteristics or operations that are at work in human beings as brain functions, that is, as functions of a material organ.

11.2.1   The language of ecclesial experience appears to maintain complete awareness of the epistemological impasse presented by any nonhistorical metaphysics. That is why it marks the boundaries of its own theology with the givens arising from of the event of the *incarnation* of God in the historical person of Jesus Christ. That which the Church "knows" about God it infers from the experience of the historical testimony of Jesus Christ as recorded by those who were eyewitnesses.

11.2.2   Language is always and inevitably relative; otherwise, it would not be language. The historical Jesus, as incarnate Son and Logos, witnesses to the Father as an existent "person" with self-consciousness, reason, thought, judgment, memory, will, and vision. But it is obvious that all these anthropomorphic signifiers are only *language*, language that refers to a reality of *relation* (of the Son to the Father, and of the Father to the world as flesh of the Son). This is a relation that is only served by concepts and images, without being subordinated to linguistic signifiers.

11.2.3   An observation made in a different mode is pertinent here. Commenting on the so-called gift of clairvoyance of certain ascetics, Isaac the Syrian notes that this is not a matter of a peculiar ability of bodily vision, yet it is clearly attested as a visual experience, as unmediated insight.[9] We do not have words in our language for the possibility of anyone "seeing" sensible events taking place in reality but without the bodily functioning of the faculty of sight. That is why in the case of the experience of clairvoyance, signifiers of a bodily function are used to signify an analogous result, empirically established, of a nonbodily function.

Perhaps similarly, in the language of the Gospels, Christ witnesses to the Father-God using linguistic signifiers that draw from the experience of the knowledge of created rational beings—he witnesses to the uncreated Father-God who is beyond beings as if witnessing to a being and a person with self-consciousness, reason, thought, judgment, memory, will, vision, and so forth.

11.2.4   Within the context of the Christian tradition, the possibility of "knowledge" of the inconceivable, invisible, incomprehensible God—the causal principle of existence—is constituted only by the experience of *relation*, relation as mode of *existence* and not simply as the product of an intellectual, emotional, intuitive, or any other kind of referential activity.

11.2.5   The experience of relation can be attested or signified by language. Language, however, is constituted by signifiers of common reference to the potentially common experience of relations with sensible and intelligible, or created, reality. By means of this common language, the experience of relation with what is beyond every sensible assertion, and beyond every intelligible, emotional, intuitive, or any other kind of anagogical ascent, can be signified or communicated—but only analogically and relatively.

The Non-sense of Comparative Religion

12 The language by which metaphysical experience is manifested or attested is subject to the relativity of epistemological apophaticism, subject to the principle of the difference between the *understanding* of signifiers and the *knowledge* of what is signified.

Apart from the relativity of the apophatic sense of the signifiers, should we perhaps accept that the *derivation* (historical, geographical, and cultural) of the signifiers imposes an additional relativity on the language of metaphysics?

Does the variety of religious traditions inevitably relativize the knowledge that is manifested or attested by the differences in the linguistic semantics of these traditions?

12.1   Is it possible for metaphysical experience, the *personal* character of the relation of human beings with the transcendent, to depend on a specific linguistic signification of the transcendent— to depend on that which defines experience as an experiential *tradition* given in local, historical, or cultural terms?

Can a *relation* with Yahweh, or Christ, or Ahura Mazda, or Allah, or Brahma be formed with the reservation that these names are relational and conventional? Can it be constituted with the certainty that the different names refer to the same single inconceivable, invisible, and incomprehensible causal principle of all that exists?

12.2   The psychological need for certainties seems to be instinctive in human beings; this is especially true of metaphysical certainties, a condition perhaps connected with the instinctive fear human beings have of the unknown. The need clothes itself in the combative conviction of religious people that their own religion is the only true one, that God's work in the world[1] is confined within the geographical and cultural boundaries of populations that embrace their "true" religion, and that the fact of the *salvation* of humankind is exhausted within those boundaries.

12.2.1   It is significant that the various religions of the world are unable to deal with this question or are even uninterested in it. Why should God show such unreasonable partiality? Why should *salvation* be a privilege only for a minority of human beings who happen—for geographical, historical, or cultural reasons—to belong to the one "true" religion? How does the God of this one "true" religion regard the billions of people who, through no fault of their own, did not, do not, and will not have a relationship with him?

Even when the Apostle Paul asserts that God has granted conscience to all human beings as a "law written on their hearts,"[2] he presupposes an elect segment of humanity that, in addition to bearing the "law of conscience," also possesses the law given by God "through Moses and the prophets" or "through faith in Jesus Christ."

On the psychological level, every religion is the only "true" one, and whoever embraces the "true" religion belongs to the "elect people of God," to a "peculiar people," to a "remnant of grace." The psychological need for metaphysical security and salvation—and this, indeed, in an exclusive sense—is instinctive in human beings.

12.2.2   It would seem perhaps anachronistic and inconsequential to look for discussions concerning the inclusion of people of a different faith in the demand for salvation in an age with a very restricted view of the planet's human geography. This does not mean that a monopolistic claim to salvation is rare today, when people have a vivid sense of being unified by instant communications. Throughout the length and breadth of the world, there exists a huge number of religious groups, sects, and charismatic assemblies, each utterly convinced that it alone preserves and represents the only genuine and authentic metaphysical truth. A few hundred or a few thousand believers, in each case, are the only ones assured of "eternal salvation," while the remaining billions of people who have ever lived on the planet, are alive now, or will live in the future are predestined to perdition.

12.3   There can be no objective comparison and evaluation of the religious experiences and traditions or propositions of the metaphysical *meaning* of reality, of the interpretation of the cause and goal of existent things. Every comparison and evaluation is based inevitably on criteria and principles of a specific epistemological and cultural paradigm.

12.3.1   If, in an oversimplified schematic fashion, we regard the ancient Greek, the more recent Western, and the modern versions of logical method as a unified epistemological paradigm (in contrast to other, mainly Eastern, theories), we would be able to put together a language capable of demonstrating (to those experienced in using the paradigm) the comparative disadvantages and comparative advantages of different *ontological* propositions of a religious or philosophical provenance.

12.3.2   It could perhaps be proved, using the strict logic of the language of the common epistemological paradigm, that the more coherent, or systematically articulated, proposals of an ontological interpretation of reality (from among those known to the Greek and Western European traditions) are the following two: a *prosopocentric ontology*, as formulated by the leading Greek exponents of the Christian ecclesial experience from the fourth to the fourteenth century; and the *nihilistic ontology* of Martin Heidegger, which has been highly representative (up to now) of the evolution of Western metaphysics.

12.3.3   The structured articulation of the logical proofs of a systematic ontology, however, cannot really be the foundational fact of subjective metaphysical experience. In metaphysics we are guided by questions that arise from our immediate relation with the physical and social reality: questions of the *meaning* (cause and purpose) of existent things and of existence itself.

12.3.4 Propositions that respond to the metaphysical questions—
that seek to constitute an ontological interpretation of reality and
to demonstrate the meaning of existence and existent things—cannot be incommunicable; they must be subject to the rules of "correct thinking in order to communicate correctly." The foundational
fact of metaphysical inquiry cannot be logic and the coherent articulation of ontological propositions; but at the same time, ontological propositions are not constituted without being subject to
the rules of logic and coherent articulation.

12.3.5 Metaphysical perception and inquiry belongs to the kind
of knowledge that becomes accessible as absolutely subjective
experience, without the knowledge's losing the pragmatism of a
communicable event. Metaphysical perception is not irrational,
nonrational, mystical, or sentimental in character. When such
perception is based on experience, rather than on imagination or
hallucination, it emerges from the existential dynamic of referenti-
ality-relation and is communicated as relation.

12.3.6 It is possible, for example, for me to understand within logically correct linguistic expressions what maternal love is. But the
only way I can *know* the reality to which the linguistic reference
maternal love refers is by the absolutely subjective relation with my
own mother.

I cannot (nor is it of any interest to attempt to do so) demonstrate or prove that my relation with my mother is "true" or that
the corresponding relation of a Chinese or a Kikuyu is less "true"
or "false." What *is* certain is that, thanks to the absolutely subjective experience of my relation with my own mother alone, I am also
able to know what the reality of maternal love is for a Chinese or a
Kikuyu.

Precisely the same assertion could be made for the knowledge
of beauty, friendship, erotic love, or God. The absolutely private
fact of subjective experience is the only possibility for realistic
knowledge of the universal and fulfilling reality of beauty, friendship, erotic love, or God.[3]

12.4   We return to the question of whether the multiplicity of
reference to—the polyonymy of—the transcendent relativizes the

reference. Are *Yahweh, Christ, Ahura Mazda, Allah*, and *Brahma*, for example, inevitably conventional signifiers and *nomina nuda* of humanity's natural, or instinctual, reference to a transcendent one and causal principle of existence?

The reservation (consciousness of relativity) can accompany the *understanding* of the linguistic reassembly of a fact of relation. It does not accompany the *knowledge* that is generated by the relation.

Every linguistic reference to maternal love and every hermeneutic analysis of this experience is relative. The knowledge of maternal love, as the absolutely subjective experience of the relationship of each of us with our own mother, is not relative.

12.4.1 Every linguistic reference to erotic love and every hermeneutic analysis of erotic experience is also relative. The erotic experience itself, as an absolutely subjective event, is knowledge that is not relative.

12.4.2 Does the multiplicity—the polyonymy—of erotic attraction relativize the reality of the erotic fact, the realistic knowledge of this fact?

The reservation (consciousness of relativity) can accompany the *understanding* of the linguistic reassembly of each partial fact of fulfilling erotic relation. It does not accompany the *knowledge* that is generated by the personal erotic relation.

12.4.3 The *name* of the beloved person is the realistic and fulfilling, nonrelativized knowledge of erotic love.

12.4.4 When does erotic love constitute knowledge, and when is it an illusion? When does knowledge constitute an eponymous reference to the transcendent, and when is it a product of the imagination? How can we distinguish, even merely by the relativity of linguistic semantics, a genuine and true relation from one that is illusory and imagined?

12.4.5 We understand the difference between erotic *attraction* and erotic *relation*: *attraction* could be signified linguistically as a fact that is experienced passively (the subject undergoes attraction, *is attracted*), is unpredictable, and is undetermined by the will (see

Plato's *exaiphnēs*, "on a sudden"[4]). *Relation* could be defined as a fact that is experienced actively (the subject participates in the relation, *relates to*); it is a fact of volitional decision, of freedom put into practice.

On the level of experience, *attraction* and *relation* are often interwoven and their difference is blunted, because the *reciprocity*, which in relations is a necessary condition, is also manifested as a result of attraction. Moreover, relation has by definition a uniqueness, whereas attraction is an experience of multiplicity (polyonymy)—although attraction frequently functions as an impression of uniqueness.

12.5   I have discussed (12.4) humanity's *natural*, or *instinctual* (multiform and polyonymous), reference to the transcendent one and causal principle of existence. We also recognize a corresponding multiformity and polyonymy in natural, or instinctual, erotic attraction, which often functions as an impression (either as a feeling or as a certainty) of uniqueness.

If both the *religious* and the *erotic* references operate primarily as instinctual operations, if they are subject to the necessity of instinct, and if they are givens of human nature, how are we to distinguish a real response from an illusory response to the human desire for *God* and for *erotic love*?

How are we to tell whether our religious and erotic references serve necessities of nature or whether they transcend the necessities of nature—whether the reference has nature as an unsurmountable limit, whether our frequent illusion that we are experiencing some ecstatic escape from nature, some transcendence of nature, is only an artifice of nature?

How can we distinguish *nature* from *relation*, *necessity* from *freedom*?

12.5.1   The criterion for making such a distinction may be indicated linguistically—always with the difference between the *understanding* of the signifiers and the *knowledge* of the things signified as a given.

We speak of a religious or erotic *relation* when the desire for the Other is activated with a volitional self-offering, an actual transcendence of the self—when it is a desire for coexistence, intercourse, communion of being. And the active reference encounters the corresponding volitional referentiality of the Other in such a way that the encounter is experienced reciprocally as an *existential* fact different from natural (individual) self-preservation.

12.5.2 We speak of reciprocity as a necessary condition for any interpersonal relation: *relation* is constituted only when the self-transcendent reference encounters the otherness of the Other as a revelation of unique intimacy and the revelation functions as a two-way dynamic.

12.5.3 We speak of religious or erotic *relation* when the desire for the Other is vitally alive: it is a desire for *life-as-relation*, a reciprocal desire, volitional and active, which consists of an existential fact—a transition to a mode of existence different from that of individual self-preservation, pleasure, or domination.

12.5.4 We speak of religious or erotic *relation* when the referentiality of desire encounters the Other *in itself*, not simply as a partner to communication, not as a step in a process to which the ego resorts in order to win recognition. The epistemic dynamic of relation is an experience of revelation: the otherness of the Other is felt palpably as a unique intimacy.

12.6   The epistemic realism of relation (relation when it produces knowledge of personal otherness) and the existential character of relation (relation when it constitutes a *mode of existence*, not an illusion) are articulations of the struggle for self-offering, self-abandonment. For that reason the following aphorism is indicative: *we know God by cultivating a relationship, not by understanding a concept*.[5]

12.6.1 The struggle for self-offering or self-abandonment is the first criterion for distinguishing whether our religious or erotic references constitute a reality of relation or an illusion of relation.

    An equally powerful criterion (always within the relativity of linguistic semantics) is that relation should consist of an achievement of freedom—that relation should not be alienated and transformed into dependence, submission, utilitarian trans-action, or convenient exploitation.

12.6.2 A term or presupposition of the truth (i.e., genuineness) of a relation must, according to the rational factors governing the sharing of our experience, be the existential integrity of the par-ticipants in the relation. If the encounter, connection, or coopera-tion of persons diminishes or inhibits the existential powers (such as the critical thought, the volitional disposition, or the creative energy) of the one and strengthens or facilitates the dominating tendencies of the other, we cannot speak of a *relation*.

12.6.3 The drive to dominate, the instinct to master, the urge to exercise an ascendancy, sadomasochism[6]—these are indicators of the alienation of the existential integrity of relational factors, indicators of the mutation of the fact of relation into an illusion of relation. And various forms of such distortions are disguised as eroticism or as religiosity.

Beauty as Invitation-to-Relation

13 What could be the real—not illusory—occasions, the experiential starting points, for a possible relation between human beings and God? Could such occasions be those when relation fulfills the following criteria: (1) implied reciprocity; (2) experiential access to the otherness of the Other; (3) transformation of an atomic mode of existence into an experience of sharing life in communion; and (4) freedom from dependence, subjection, utilitarian transaction, or convenient exploitation?

13.1   Let us exclude from the outset as nonreal occasions or invalid starting points of relation: (1) the purely intellectual hypothesis (*suppositio*) of the existence of God, even if it is inferred from arguments of high apodictic (methodological) validity; and (2) that which we could call a *psychological certainty*: the instinctive kinds of certainties which are "secreted" by our psychological makeup in order to compensate for unconscious fears and insecurities—the kinds of certainties that are registered in experience as reflecting displeasure or pleasure, discomfort or comfort.

13.2   Given the analogies in common experience between erotic relation and relation with God, the likewise common experience of beauty offers indications of a real (not illusory) occasion or starting point for both of these possible kinds of relation.

13.2.1 How could we define *beauty*? Is it the socially defined grades of what is pleasing? Is it a non-predetermined subjective enjoyment? Is it a feeling of psychological indeterminacy? Is it a quality subject to measurable features?

We have no adequate support for linking, according to naturalist precepts, the perception or experience of beauty either with the satisfaction of primordial urges (for self-preservation, for example—urges that precede even the defensive reflexes of discontent and contentment) or with stimuli reducible to sexual pleasure.

13.2.2 The experience of beauty always has a sensible (i.e., arising from the senses) starting point, but not all information coming from the senses is an experience of beauty. This statement leads to the following questions.

First, what is the factor, the experiential element or criterion, that "translates" certain information conveyed by the senses into an experience of beauty?

Second, what common element renders a particular sight, a particular sound, a particular sensation of touch, smell, or taste an experience of beauty?

And the most difficult question of all: what element imparts beauty to a product of the human mind—an image, a piece of music, or a linguistic utterance (spoken or written, in poetry or in prose)? What criterion permits us to distinguish "high" art from juvenile products, the gifted artist from one who is simply untalented?

13.2.3 The common element of every experience of beauty—experience mediated by vision, hearing, touch, taste, or smell—is not necessarily morphic; that is, it is not related to the measure, the style, the proportions, the arrangement, or the construction of the thing perceived. Such elements do not distinguish a good smell from a bad one, sweet from sour, roughness from smoothness or delicacy. Nor can beauty necessarily be identified with (nor is it exhausted by) the pleasure it gives to the senses; for to which of the senses does a work of literature, for example, or a poem, appeal?

13.2.4 The volitional element could perhaps be proposed as a common denominator of every experience of beauty: beauty *charms*, that is to say, it attracts, it stimulates the desire for relation, for participation, for communion, for intercourse. A term which would locate beauty in the dynamics of the power to charm seems compatible with common experience and potentially fruitful. This dynamics of the *invitation-to-relation* also preserves the absolute otherness by which beauty is internalized as a subjective experience. It preserves, too, the indeterminacy of the natural gift (or talent), which distinguishes the charm of the products of human skill or the decisive contribution made by the education, training, and ethos of the artist.

13.2.5   If we accept *charm* (*thelxis*) as a definition of beauty, beauty as *invitation-to-relation*, then we attribute to the subjective experience of beauty the dynamics of the steps of an indeterminate ladder—a dynamics precisely analogous to the experience of relation. Beauty, like every experience of relation, may be experienced on various levels ranging from hedonistic self-containedness to the most complete self-transcendence. Beauty may be internalized as an invitation to individualistic pleasure, as a desire to appropriate and possess that which charms, but it may also be internalized on the infinity of intermediate levels leading up to the attainment of freedom from the necessities of egocentric urges.

13.2.6   The way we estimate the degree of success in the expression of a creative artist's personal otherness through the *logos* of his or her art (the linguistic, musical, or representational *logos*) is similar to this. The more *erotic* the *logos* of the artist is (that is, the more it manifests transcendence and invites to relationship), the more fully it formulates its personal otherness, its uniqueness and dissimilarity. In the individualistic culture of modernity, many attempts at artistic creation spring from an obvious weakness or denial of *relation* (the artist's relation with the material of the art and with the participant in the work of the art), from a weakness or denial of the struggle for self-transcendence that lends a social dynamic to the art. The unrelated linguistic, musical, or representational *logos* serves exclusively, and becomes immediately obvious as, the artist's ego; that is to say, the unrelated *logos* gives priority to the impression (the effect) that the work will create, the originality of the technique, the provoking of individual emotions, the stimulation of pleasurable well-being, the display of technical coherence—it serves not the sharing of experience or the invitation-to-relation but the work of art itself, the grounds for attracting admiring attention to the artist's uncommunicated ego.

13.3   The beauty of nature offers indications of real—not illusory—grounds for a possible realization of a *relation* between humanity and a personal causal principle of existence: between humanity and a rational God, a God-Logos. I repeat that beauty never functions in an obligatory fashion as charm, a starting point of relation, and that which functions as charm is never an objective (true for everyone) reality of beauty.

13.3.1   A juicy, fragrant, tasty piece of fruit, the shapes and colors of flowers in spring, a striking landscape, a sunset with a riot of colors can each be an experience of beauty. One can ignore such an experience as a self-evident natural fact, a result of chance. One can internalize the experience as a transient moment of aesthetic pleasure, its cause unexplained. Such an experience can function "on a sudden" as an immediate personal sense of gift, an immediacy of perception that someone offers this gift to reveal an invitation-to-relation or even his "manic love" for the recipient.

13.3.2   "Be mindful of me, beloved maiden," the poet writes of the woman who invites to dinner him whom her heart has chosen. And she prepares the choicest foods she can find. She lays a festive table, decorates it with embroideries and flowers, lights candles in silver candlesticks so as to say, silently and discreetly, to him she has invited, "I love you, I am in love with you." The recipient either decodes the signifiers of his reception, or more probably, "slow of heart," he dines and enjoys himself without the slightest inkling of the motives and the purpose of the invitation.

13.3.3   For the language of beauty to be "read" as invitation-to-relation what is required, rather, is a non-predetermined readiness—at least, a readiness not subject to suggestions, incitements, arguments. This readiness could be described as *erotic*, if by *eros* we mean assent to the struggle to attain self-abandonment and self-offering. At any rate, for the experience of physical beauty to function referentially, to refer to the personal immediacy of God the Creator, to be "read" as an erotic summons from God the Lover and Bridegroom of humankind, the decisive factor cannot be some rational proof of the significance of beauty, nor the deceptive persuasion of emotional excitement. Objective beauty (i.e., beauty "lying opposite me") manifests the dynamic of a personal invitation to a personal relation in the field of non-predeterminacy, where every reality of *relation* is either generated or not generated, and in the latter case where the ego's carapace is not shattered.

There will always be people who will live their one unique life without ever encountering Mozart, Van Gogh, or Cavafy—without a language of musical, artistic, or poetic beauty ever functioning for them "on a sudden" as an erotic invitation to participate in the personal otherness—the uniqueness and dissimilarity—of the composer, the artist, or the poet.

13.3.4   More perhaps than the experience of erotic love, beauty as charm confirms relation as a possible mode of existence that is not subject to predeterminations of nature—it permits us to speak of a *relational ontology*. Erotic desire for life-as-relation is easily confused with the unconscious disguises assumed by the sex drive. In the case of beauty, however, even if charm functions according to the laws of natural desire, communion, or intercourse (how else would existence as enhypostasized in nature function?), the charm of beauty remains free from subjection to the predeterminations and necessities of nature.

Nonbeauty, or the Problem of Evil

14 The beauty of nature, as well as every experience of beauty, has a dynamic referentiality, always in correlation with the readiness of the recipient to refer to the invitatory *logos* of beauty. As otherness of *logos*, every manifestation of natural beauty refers to, or points to, the existential otherness of a creator as Person (just as a painting points to the artist and a piece of music to the composer). Accordingly, the beauty of nature constitutes a real, not illusory, starting point for a possible realization of humanity's relationship with a personal causal principle of existence: with a rational God, a God-Logos.

Yet nature is not only a reality of *beauty*; it is also a reality of *nonbeauty*: it functions not only as *invitation-to-relation*, as charm, but also as exclusion (either progressive or sudden) of the rational subject from every relation. Nature functions, that is to say, as the imposition of irresistible necessities on the rational subject—an imposition that excludes choice or freedom, and therefore relation. Nature functions as a law of decay, pain, torment, and finally extinction (death of physical existence) that governs the rational subject. Nature functions, in consequence, not only as charm but also as repulsion, as repudiation, as the sense of a threat directed toward humanity, as a source of fear.

The reality (and also the threat) of the decay, pain, or death of our rational existence is defined by us human beings with a single word: *evil*.

14.1   Beauty summons to relation, but evil is of itself nonbeautiful: it repels, it frightens, it threatens.

Beauty possesses an otherness of invitatory *logos*, and thus also a dynamic referentiality: it refers, or points, to (potentially) the existential otherness of its rational causal principle. Evil also has a rational otherness, at least formally; every case or threat of decay, pain, or death is unique and dissimilar. Does evil, too, refer, or point, to an existential otherness of its rational causal principle?

14.1.1   The rational otherness—the indeterminate circumstantial polymorphy—of evil is repulsive, not charming, and as necessitude excludes the realization of reference as *relation*. We can identify the referentiality of evil either as a merely noetic tracing of effects to their logical causes or even as an experiential confirmation of an undetermined rational factor that contrives the polymorphy of the circumstantial manifestations of evil. The *personification* of evil in almost every religious tradition is not outside the mode of human rationality.

14.2   In the realm of systematic thought (the methodical formulations that permit the fuller communication of experience), the initial questions that the existence of evil provokes are three: (1) Does evil really have a causal principle? (2) Is the causal principle of evil different from the causal principle of beauty? (3) Could that which human beings experience as evil be a misinterpreted aspect of the very *invitation-to-relation* that is manifested by beauty?

14.2.1   Following what has been established empirically and its logical or referential dynamic, the human rational subject could perhaps accept two causal principles of physical reality, two engendering factors woven together into the existential fact that are antithetical and actively hostile to each other. The first is a causal factor, which through the beauty or wisdom of nature invites the rational subject to a rational (and perhaps also existential) *relation* with it. The second is an unrelated factor (beyond rational relation and empirically accessible only as existential anti-reason), which imposes the decay, suffering, and death of the rational subject as a necessity.

14.2.2 The acceptance of such a position would be logically coherent—that is, consistent with the rules of "correct thinking"—and
supported in the indicative referentiality of common experience.
It is a position, however, that discusses causation without offering
an explanation of natural beauty or natural evil and, consequently,
fails to solve any problem: it creates a hermeneutic void that abol-
ishes any *sense* in the existential fact, that strips the existential fact
of goal or purpose. Such an argument obliges us to view human
rational existence as the nonsensical victim of an irrational play of
enigmatic supernatural factors, which square up against each other
on the level of a cosmic reality constituted with supreme wisdom.

14.3   In the course of history, the human capacity for rational
thought has formed propositions for the explanation of evil—ex-
planations of evil's inherent presence in the existential fact as the
human rational subject recognizes it and experiences it. The following cases, briefly treated here, provide illustrative examples.

14.3.1   First, in the case of ancient Greek thought, one may infer
from a broad range of brilliantly expressed ideas a common, self-
evident reception or perception of evil, although this is formulated
only in an indirect, nondeliberate way.
    The ancient Greek perception seems to have located evil "on-
tologically" in matter itself, before matter has been invested with
form, or *logos*—before its *eidopoiēsis* or *logopoiēsis*—that is, before
logos, or reason, has endowed the matter with form or shape (*eidos-
morphē*) and rendered it a participant in existence.
    Only by the *logos* of the form does an existent thing participate
in existence—the essence (*ousia*) of a being (an *on*) is the *logos*
or mode of its participation in being (in *to einai*). The logoi, or
principles, of beings (unexplained givens) and the equally given,
common (*xynos*) *logos* of the universal formation of existent things
are the real causes of being. Without the morphic, or differentiat-
ing, *logos*, the principle that procures form, nothing participates
in existence: amorphousness, the lack of form, the lack of shape or
schema,[1] was for the Greeks synonymous with nonexistence.
    At the same time, *logos*—the essences, the forms of existent
things, and the common principle of the order of the universe—is

the permanent, stable, incorruptible, changeless, immortal eternal given, and consequently that which really exists, the really real (*to ontōs on*), the true, the good. By contrast, matter in itself before its investment with form and reason (therefore by definition identical with nonexistence and empirically verified as corruptible, mutable, and transient) is that which is really evil.

If such an interpretation of evil has been correctly based on the evidence of Greek thought and art, it certainly excites respect for its logical consistency, though not for its hermeneutic adequacy. The reality of decay, pain, sickness, and death, and also of injustice, hatred, exploitation, and denigration (whether given in nature or attributable to the passions of human evil) remain unexplained in the ancient Greek perspective. Indeed, this latter reality of "moral evil," as it was later called, was regarded by the Greeks as an existential category so self-evidently given that it was attributed without scruple even to the gods: if the gods *exist*, then they surely hate, are at enmity, are scheming, take revenge, and utter lies. They are, however, free from the "natural evils" of decay, sickness, and death.

14.3.2 A second illustrative attempt at an ontological interpretation of evil can be traced in the philosophy of Plotinus.

Plotinus was the first to attribute the reality of evil to the autonomy and freedom of humankind. His hermeneutic theories take their origin from certain ontological positions accepted by Plato: before it was mingled with the body, the human soul preexisted in the supracelestial realm of the logoi (ideas or models) of every existent thing and was itself the radiance and image of that intellectual place that Plotinus identifies with Intellect, or *Nous*. *Nous* for Plotinus is identified with the Demiurge of whom Plato speaks in the *Timaeus* and also with Aristotle's God, who is "thought thinking itself": *Nous* emanates from the transcendent *One* (ungraspable by the intellect, ineffable, beyond all essence), just as rays of light emanate from the sun.

The human soul is a type of the universal *Nous* and participates in its noetic essence, from which it has "fallen." The fall of the soul is a given fact, and consequently there is also a prelapsarian phase of its existence. What is the cause of the fall? In an early hermeneutic essay, Plotinus attributes the fall of the soul to a form of weakness, a diminution of strength and of its active powers, which is provoked by its admixture with matter, its combining with the body; it is as if matter "steals" existential space, existential powers, from the soul, as if matter appropriates the soul's existential space and, consequently, transforms it into evil (since evil by definition is matter).[2]

In a second, more developed, hermeneutic essay, Plotinus locates the cause of the fall in the wrong use of the gift of independence and freedom that the human soul (as image and radiance of the *Nous*) possesses. By "coming into matter," souls do not cease to act in the mode of the *Nous*: they endow matter with form, or shape, or *logos*—that is to say, souls *create* existent things. Thus, they delight in the independence and freedom of their activities; they are constantly emboldened to achieve greater freedom of operation; they slip into existential self-sufficiency, into the desire for autonomy, the desire to belong only to themselves. They forget where they have come from; they value, admire, and wonder at all that they themselves do; they attach themselves to the things that are within the world; by causing a rupture, souls distance themselves from their own self and origin.[3]

14.3.3 A third proposal for an ontological interpretation of evil was shaped by the Christian tradition, which also borrowed from the Hebrew Scriptures (the Christian Old Testament) a number of archetypal images, symbols, linguistic expressions, and conventions.

We could summarize the Christian proposal as three specific theses.

(a) Universal reality (the sum total of existent things) is the product created ex nihilo of the uncreated energies of the one triadic God. The cause of creation is solely the love of God, his free wish to share his existential fullness with beings created in his image. For this reason, he created everything as "very good"; the logoi of beings are manifestations of the invitation-to-relation that God by his creative act addresses to humanity. There is no evil "according to essence" in the divine creation—"God is not the creator of evil."[4]

(b) That which we call *evil* is a consequence of behavior, of the will, not a reality of nature or essence. In order that humanity's response to God's invitation of love be positive and loving, a freedom of existential self-determination is presupposed, as is, consequently, the possibility that humanity would reject God's invitation, would prefer the existential autonomy, or self-containedness, of its created nature—with all that this autonomy entails. Pain, toil, decay, death, and every other manifestation of evil are the existential deficiency that created being exhibits when it rejects existing in the mode of the uncreated—that is, in the mode of love.[5]

(c) In its existential self-determination, humanity may be influenced by rational, personal beings of a "spiritual" (immaterial) nature, beings that preceded the world in God's creation and freely chose to rebel, to break with God, to reject a relationship with God—they chose an existential self-determination of rivalry and hostility with respect to the love of God. These beings are created by God, and therefore their nature is also "very good," but by their free will they choose denial, or evil. They "tempt" humanity; they try to make it share in their rebellion.

14.3.4 The Christian Church—at least, the undivided Church of the first few centuries—endeavored, as a rule, to express itself in language that referred to historical experience. A characteristic formulation is: "We declare to you . . . what we have heard, what we have seen with our eyes, what we have looked at and touched with our hands."[6]

Such an approach places a consistent emphasis on the realism of a linguistic expression that signifies or manifests the experience of the ecclesial community and is verified and attested by the experience itself. In its modes of expression, the Church avoided any recourse to *a priori* (merely intellectual, experientially unconfirmed) affirmations, any use of autonomous rational argument, any appeal to axiomatic (empirically not subject to demonstration) "principles," any claim that particular linguistic formulations (to do with God's intervention in the shaping of terminology and the construction of a human linguistic idiom) possessed a transcendent validity. The Church adhered consistently to the apophatic character of the linguistic formulations of its experience, refusing to exhaust the truth in its formulation or to identify the knowledge of the things signified merely with the understanding of the signifiers.

The apophaticism of the Church's language is unavoidably interconnected with the relativity of whatever happen to be the prevailing opinions in each phase of its historical and cultural evolution—with the relativity of the scientific world picture, or of the social ideas of any given time, or of the current political models. Both these factors—*apophaticism* and the *historical relativity* of the linguistic code—shape the language of each historical period. Their combination, however, perhaps permits (or favors) the creation, in the later stages of historical and cultural development, of important gaps in the hermeneutic fullness of the fundamental propositions of the Christian witness.

It is likely that today, at the beginning of the twenty-first century, the most characteristic instance of such hermeneutic gaps will be found in the propositions of the Church's witness that relate to the decoding of the enigma of evil.

Intermezzo on Natural Religion

15 The Church's reliance on the apophatic character of the linguistic formulations of its experience also differentiates it from any kind of "natural religion."[1] We need to dwell on this fundamental point of difference before we attempt to approach the logical space (as an experientially verifiable semantics) of the propositions of the Christian interpretation of evil—to approach them on the basis of the modern scientific worldview.

15.1 We call *natural religion* the many forms of collective faith, worship, and morality which derive from the natural, or instinctive, need of human beings to protect themselves from the transcendent unknown and ward off its influence with regard to powers and factors that determine the existence and self-preservation of human beings but do not come under the control of their will.

15.1.1 We call *faith*, within the context of natural religion, the intellectual submission of the individual to axiomatic (undemonstrable) principles of the interpretation of reality with the aim of encasing the ego in the certainties of convictions together with an accompanying sense of authoritative validity.

15.1.2 Within the same context, we call *worship* the practical means devised by human beings for propitiating—for influencing favorably with regard to themselves as individuals—unknown and hypothetically metaphysical powers that occupy the role of a causal principle of what exists or takes place in the world. It is an instinctive human need to win the sympathy of these powers (by sacrifices and other ritual actions), to avert their unpredictable "anger," to align the powers with one's desires for protection, for help with the inconveniences of daily life, for guaranteeing immortality for one's own ego.

15.1.3   *Morality*, finally, still within the context of natural religion, is the codified objectification of regulative principles of behavior, an objectification that is regarded as a law of absolute validity given by God himself and that ensures that the individual receives a guaranteed certainty of obedience to the divine will. The more detailed and circumstantial the moral code, the more precisely measurable is certainty concerning the individual's virtue, merit, and assurance of eternal reward.

15.2   A fundamental mark of natural, or instinctual, religion is its *individualistic* character—its enclosure within the needs and necessities that govern the biological individual. And an instinctive individualism is not (as one might logically expect) accompanied by an extreme relativism. Quite the contrary, instinctive individualism is accompanied by an insatiable pursuit of objectivity, because only objective certainties, objective assertions and calculations, offer the individual support and security, render the individual impervious to doubt, invest the individual with authority, assertiveness, and executive power.

15.3   From the first moments of its historical presence, the Christian Church has stood at the pole opposite to natural religion.

The Christians adopted the Greek noun *ecclēsia* to manifest their identity, the reality of an assembly constituted not on the basis of common convictions, moral aims, or utilitarian goals but on the foundation of the struggle to realize a mode of existence.

The word *ecclēsia* referred to the historical experience of ancient Greece, where citizens came together in the *ecclēsia of the dēmos*, the assembly of the people, in order to realize and manifest the *city*, that mode of coexistence designed to promote a rational harmony and order of social relations—that is to say, the common (*xynos*) *logos* of universal order, an immutable, incorruptible, eternal *logos*-mode, and therefore a paradigm of "real existence," of true being.

The experience of the Christian Church, an experience of the historical presence and witness of Jesus of Nazareth, recognizes as a mode of "real existence" not the uninterpreted cosmic rationality but the relations of Persons who constitute the triadic causal principle of being. This existential mode is love (*agapē*) as unconditional freedom. The Church is described as a *body* with an organic and vital unity of members, within which one participates in life as a struggle to share love, a struggle to attain a mode of existence.

15.3.1 The very identity of the Church is manifested as being by definition incompatible with any form of individualism, any individualistic intentionality. Participation in the ecclesial fact signifies an attempt, an ascetic struggle, to divest oneself of egotistic priorities. On almost every page of the Gospels, which record the experience and witness of the first ecclesial community, that which is individual, or atomic, is identified with death—atomic religiosity, atomic virtue, atomic convictions—and that which is shared with love is unbounded life, real being, and truth.

15.3.2 The struggle to transcend the focus on the individual also includes the rejection of any demand for *objectivity*. In the texts of the Gospels, any objective grading or evaluating of religiosity, virtue, or piety is overturned and rejected: those convinced that they are justified by their own efforts—the observers of the Law, the "first" on a measurable standard of devotion to God—prove to be "last" in the fact of true life. Those who have genuinely renounced any public esteem or confidence in themselves—the tax collectors, the prostitutes, the robbers, the prodigal—prove to be the ones forging ahead in proportion to their readiness to abandon themselves to God's love and nothing else.[2] From the same gospel perspective, the Apostle Paul battles in his Epistles against that supreme objective support for religious individualism: the Law.[3]

15.4 It is with the same aim—namely, the transcendence of individualism—that the Christian Church also refuses *to objectify its truth*: there is no objective source of truth for the Church, no authentic formulation, no dogmatic code, no system of principles.

The Church's truth cannot be transformed into an epistemic object accessible only to individual understanding, subject to being possessed and mastered by the individual intellect. The Church's truth is recognized—it becomes accessible and known—only by the experience of participation in the ecclesial fact, and this not in a mystical or emotional manner but by the mode of *relation*, just as we approach every empirical reality: by the knowledge of maternal affection, the knowledge of erotic love, the knowledge of the revelations of art.

15.4.1 The texts of the Gospels, the written memoirs of the proclamation of the first apostolic community; the Epistles of the Apostles; and the writings of the great teachers and Fathers of the ecclesial body are of the utmost value to the Church and are to be respected as such. These texts record the Church's experience, interpret it, and initiate us into or lead us toward this experience. But the texts are not substitutes for the truth of the Church, nor are they identical with it. Something analogous is the case with any written (objectified) reference—even the most talented or the most poetic—to maternal affection, erotic love, or the revelations of art.

15.4.2 The linguistic signing or marking of ecclesial experience—that is, its witness and proclamation—has very often been distorted, falsified, twisted in the course of history. And this distortion, falsification, twisting has been pursued in order to change the meaning of ecclesial experience (evidently by expressing the alienation of the experience *itself*).

In the first eight centuries of Christian life, the distortion of the Christian gospel through a large number of heresies was identified and condemned by the common consciousness and experience of the members of the ecclesial body. The clarity of this experience functioned as a standard and criterion for confirming heresy.

When a heresy reached the point of threatening to confuse the standards and criteria of ecclesial experience, the bishops of the local churches came together in *synods*, or *councils*, either provincial or general, that is, ecumenical. There each bishop expressed not his own private opinion, wisdom, or virtuous understanding but the experience of the body over which he had been appointed to preside.

The formulations in which the *catholic* ecclesial experience (the experience of the *katholou*—the entire, integral, unimpaired—fact of the Church) found its fullest possible expression were adopted as the decisions of the councils. These decisions were called the synodical *horoi* ("boundaries," and hence "definitions"); they were accepted not as ideological, axiomatic principles but as *boundaries,* or *boundary markers*, of the Church's experiential truth.

15.4.3   One can understand the definitions of the Church councils—likewise the Gospels and the writings of the Fathers—without *coming to know* the Church's truth, without gaining experience of its truth, just as one can understand or memorize the rules of swimming or cycling without knowing how to swim or ride a bicycle.

Truth is not to be identified with its linguistic formulations; language only marks, or signifies, the intellectual boundaries of truth. The guardian and keeper of truth can only be the social body with experience of the truth.

15.5   The empirical knowledge of the Church's truth presupposes a struggle to transcend the self, a participation in relations of communion. By contrast, an instinctive religiosity is tied to humanity, and its needs are compelling. Consequently, religiosity inevitably undermines the ecclesial struggle and tends to replace it. The *heresies*, which appeared from the start in the Church's historical life, were, as a rule, formal expressions of religious needs; they sought to replace shared empirical knowledge with the individual assurance and security of intellectual comprehension. They bypassed the priority of the ecclesial fact, favoring an *ideological* version of Christianity, its "religionization."

15.5.1   The Church's consciousness resisted the religionization of Christianity for at least eight centuries—not without inconsistencies, compromises, and retreats. Nevertheless, the people of the Church in those years were still able to distinguish pseudo-synods from synods that expressed the ecclesial experience; they were still able to distinguish the "Fathers," or begetters, in the Church's life from the ideologues (often highly talented) of a "Christian" religious intellectualism.

Monasticism in those centuries was still in the vanguard of the ecclesial struggle: it constituted a practical witness consistent with the priority of experience, the priority of self-denial for participation and sharing in relations of communion with truth. In comparison with the intellectual certainties, which strengthen the ego, the ascetic experience of the monk was an "unknowing," but *an unknowing beyond all knowledge*. Monasticism refused to cash in the fruits of ascetic self-denial for an objective, worldly authority.

The clergy—bishops, presbyters, and deacons—played a corresponding role. They seemed at that time to have preserved the sense that they were serving the ecclesial fact, the realization and manifestation of a "new" mode of sharing in existence—not serving individual religious needs. Perhaps that is why they did not seek to be called by religious titles, such as *priest* and *chief priest*.

15.5.2   The historical truth is that gradually, religionization prevailed, that the ecclesial consciousness became restricted to minorities or, in certain periods, only to certain groups. And together with a host of other symptoms, the worship of objectivity both in faith and in morality came to prevail.

Objective sources of Christian truth were sought out: records or institutional expressions of incontrovertible validity. The texts witnessing to the experience of the Apostles were identified as "authentic" documents, were described as "sacred" writings or "Holy Scripture." In order to underscore the certainty of the objectively infallible interpretation of these texts, the inferred historical continuity of the institutions that ensured hermeneutic correctness and that were described as ecclesiastical "Tradition" was mobilized as a second source of Christian truth.

15.5.3   When the misuses (and abuses) of the prerogatives arising from the exercise of authority that "Tradition" had guaranteed to ecclesiastical institutions had become excessive, the Protestant Reformation arose, a movement that denied this second source of truth and declared that "Scripture alone" (*sola scriptura*) was sufficient. The text of Scripture was idolized: it was regarded as *divinely inspired*—that is to say, it had been dictated to the authors directly by God, word for word, even down to the punctuation. Thus Christians can have immediate individual access—without the mediation of institutions and a priesthood—to truth, can possess it and exercise authority over it, just as their instinctive religious need demands.

15.5.4   A corresponding idolization of "Tradition" was offered by Roman Catholicism to its adherents. In this case the access of the individual to truth (the atomic possession of and authority over truth) is guaranteed by a disciplined obedience to the "infallible ca-thedra" of the bishop of Rome. He is God's representative (*vicarius*) on earth, and his official pronouncements have the objective as-surance of transcendent authority. When Christians are faithful to the declarations and commands of the Roman see, they know with certainty that they possess the truth and have authority over it, just as their instinctive religious need demands.

15.5.5   A double idolization, that of Scripture and Tradition, is of-fered to its own adherents by "Orthodoxism," a religionized version of the Orthodox Catholic Church, a Church that for centuries had resisted alienation, only to succumb finally to Western European culture and its cognate religionization of the Church. In its search for an ideological feature that would differentiate it from Roman Catholicism and Protestantism, Orthodoxism professes to repre-sent the "middle way" between the extremities of the other two branches of Christianity. That is to say, it idolizes both Scripture and Tradition, identifying Tradition not with the representation of truth by only one (infallible) see but with the infallibility of all the decisions and canons of the Ecumenical Councils, all the writings of the Fathers, the form of worship, and every quirk of custom, even down to the composition of the calendar and the list of feasts. Thus Orthodox Christians have a host of idols to worship, many objecti-fied "truths," which are put forward so that their psychological egos can possess them and exercise authority over them, just as their instinctive religious need demands.

15.5.6   Before an approach to the logical space—empirically veri-fiable in its semantics—of the propositions of a Christian interpretation of evil can be attempted, criteria (and watchfulness) are demanded that make possible a clear distinction between the Church and natural religion. That is to say, what is demanded is a consistent withdrawal from idolized authorities: axiomatic principles, supernatural "revelations," dogmatic *a priori* assertions. A typical mark of natural, or instinctual, religiosity is the schematic objectification of "good" and of "evil," the need to locate evil definitively in every situation (with a view to "exorcising" it).

Here what is important is that we should draw near (so far as possible) to the empirical assurances by which the specific identity of the ecclesial mode of existence is coordinated (not contradicted)—assurances that are usually attested by ecclesial experience in a symbolic, or iconic, language or (what is more difficult) in a language that is drawn from the *endoxa* (the reputable ideas, or the scientifically established facts) of every age.

Uncertainty about Evil

"In every serious problem uncertainty reaches into the roots of the problem."

—Ludwig Wittgenstein
Bemerkungen über die Farben 3, 44

16 Ecclesial experience sees in the world, in its reality as a whole, the creative activity (ex nihilo) of a personal Creator. It encounters in the world the *logos* of the personal otherness of its Creator—precisely in the way we discover the *logos* of the artist in his painting or of the composer in his music.

16.1   The recognition of the *logos* of personal otherness as the creative cause of the world cannot be obligatory; it does not constitute proof of the existence of a Creator. For anyone to recognize in a piece of music the creative otherness of the *logos* that points to the person of Mozart, a relation or familiarity with this *logos* is presupposed, an achievement of logical encounter with the creator. The encounter and relation cannot be forced by proofs.

16.2   Within the perspective opened up by the ecclesial mode of the relation of humanity with material reality, the world is not an objective *what* but an active *how*; it is not a sum total of given entities but a sum total of active relations.

16.2.1 Relations of *rational qualities*, relations of units of energy, constitute the reality of the world from its smallest to its greatest dimensions. These are relations of mode of rational harmony, order, and beauty; they reflect a *logos*, "a well-arranged musical harmony,"[1] summoning to *relation*: the rational consciousness of the world (humanity) is called to *relation* with the creator God-Logos.

16.2.2 The invitatory character of the rationality of the world hints—always within the perspective of ecclesial experience—at the *meaning* (cause and purpose) of the world, and at *love* as God's mode of existence and operation, or energy, as the freedom of his will to share his existential fullness with beings created *in his image*.

16.3   The world is the created result of God's uncreated energy, an existential fact entirely different from its existential cause. Yet there is also an active *logos* of God. (An experiential analogy, again, is the artist's painting, which is an existential given entirely different—in its nature and essence—from the artist's being, and yet an active *logos* manifesting the artist's personal uniqueness.)

16.3.1 God is uncreated; the world is created. This difference is determined linguistically as being prior to the distinctions of nature or essence.

16.4   The human intellect understands the *uncreated* as free from any existential predetermination, and the *created* as subject to prescriptions and predeterminations of its existence and therefore to necessities restrictive of existence. Temporality, spatiality, decay, and death are such necessities restrictive of the existence of created being. Universal human experience throughout time confirms that every existential given of the world's reality (most apparent in animate being) has a temporal beginning and a temporal end, is spatially dimensional, decays, and dies.

16.4.1 Temporal and spatial limitation, decay, and death are—for universal human experience throughout time—negative predeterminations of existence; they constitute evil. The Church's witness, however, is coordinated from the outset with a teaching it received from the Jewish tradition, its historical matrix: God created all things "very good,"[2] and evil cannot be inherent in God's creation—cannot be an expression of createdness, an expression of materiality. "God is not the creator of evil."[3]

16.4.2 If the cause of creation is only the love of God—that is, his free wish to share his existential fullness with beings created "in his image"—then the cause of evil must be located in a factor subsequent to creation. The Church's tradition locates the cause of evil in humanity's freedom.

16.4.3 The proposed hermeneutic schema says that we do not know the causal principle of what exists; it lies outside the boundaries of our epistemic capacities, for it eludes our ability to grasp or comprehend it (i.e., the causal principle is *aperinoētē* and *akatalēptē*). We establish it indirectly as the otherness of the creative *logos* of the things in the world that are givens, a *logos* that points to what our experience recognizes as a *personal* being (a being with self-consciousness, rationality, freedom of action). The world is the language by which God is witnessed and by which he invites humanity to a vital relation with him, by which he invites humanity to share in his mode of real existence and life. The possibility of responding to the invitation of God's love also presupposes (interprets) humanity's self-consciousness, rationality, and freedom of action, or freedom of existential self-determination—that humanity should be able to accept but also reject the invitation of God's love. Rejection signifies the repudiation of a loving relation as a mode of existence, the repudiation of the possibility that the created human being should exist in the mode of the uncreated God—the mode of freedom from time, space, decay, and death. Therefore, by its rejection, humanity repudiates the possibility of immortality and chooses existential self-containedness and autonomy for created being: existential restrictions and death are introduced into God's creation. The cause, then, of evil is to be located in human freedom.

16.4.4 This hermeneutic proposition is vulnerable on three points:
     (a) It presupposes that in the interval between the appearance of animate beings and the emergence of rational human life, there

is no natural death (no natural *reality* of death); that death (the definitive cessation of all biological functions of a vegetal or animal organism) appeared in animate nature at a time later than the emergence of humankind. Scientific study and research have established that such a presupposition cannot be true. That death has always belonged to the "biocycle"[4] of organic matter is a concomitant of its appearance from the beginning. Death has always been a necessary condition for the functioning of the food chain,[5] and consequently for the entire ecosystem. It was also always a presupposition for the functioning of the law of natural selection, which governs the dynamic of the evolution of species.[6]

(b) The above hermeneutic proposition presupposes a unified (inclusive of everyone) refusal of human beings to respond to the invitation-to-relation that God addresses to each of us personally. Such a presupposition is historically without evidence and lacks rational consistency.

The possibility that the refusal has been transmitted by inheritance, that it should be located in an original "protoplast" couple from whom the whole of the human race has descended and who have passed on their refusal to their descendants like a disease or a genetic code, likewise cannot be true, for several reasons.

First, the refusal of a relationship, the result of an act of will, is a rational operation, and if rational operations were transmitted by inheritance (by biological necessity), then the very reality of the rational subject would be abolished, as would the capacity for non-predetermined exercise of the will, choices of one's own volition, and active otherness.

Second, if we suppose that the consequences of an "original" or "ancestral" decision of the will are transmitted by inheritance, that is, biologically (like some kind of urge or instinct, analogous to inherited artistic tendencies), the hermeneutic gap remains: we will continue to account for decay and death as biological effects of an act of the will and, indeed, as effects not reversible by a contrary act of the will.

Third, the origin of the human species from one original pair endowed with rational capacities is a view disputed (with objections supported by evidence) by contemporary scientific research.

Fourth, if decay and death are universal for the human race as a consequence of a single individual originating act—a consequence that is irreversible, irrevocable, and irreparable, regardless of the individual will and responsibility of every rational subject—then this is equivalent to an absurd and sadistic existential condemnation, incompatible with the "very good" character of God's creation.

Fifth, the hermeneutic absurdity is extended further if this condemnation of the whole human race is regarded as transmitted in consequence of guilt for a single original choice by individuals who were literally at a primordial stage of development: a stage of inexperience, ignorance, unexercised intelligence, and untested critical capacity.

(c) The above hermeneutic scheme comes into conflict with the certainties, universally accepted by modern physicists, that are entailed by the second law of thermodynamics: *the principle of entropy.* According to this principle, living organisms (macroscopic bodies with an internal structure) are thermic systems open to the assumption of energy and its conversion, a fact that increases the *entropy* (the state of disorder) of the system, resulting in its tendencies to restore equilibrium (entropic balance) by means of functional structures of high organization—but also resulting in thermodynamic death as its final conclusion.

The "Fall" and the "Reputable Opinions" of Different Ages

17 The Christian tradition did not form its own proposal for a causal explanation of evil. It borrowed and developed an archetypal language of images, symbols, and personifications from the sacred Scriptures of the Jewish people (what Christians call the Old Testament).

17.1   In the text of the four Gospels (written memoirs of the proclamation, or kerygma, of the first apostolic community), there is no reference to the "fall" of humanity—to a protoplast pair of human beings who sinned against God and whose sin weighed as an inheritance on the whole human race. There is, however, frequent reference to the self-evident *sin* or *sins* of every human being,[1] to degrees of sinfulness,[2] and to the possibility that one can sin not only against one's *brother*, that is, one's *neighbor*,[3] but also against *heaven*.[4]

17.1.1   There are also frequent references to a personified evil: to the *devil* (*diabolos*, "slanderer"), who is also characterized as the *tempter*, *Satan* ("adversary"), and *Beelzebub*—a popular name in Palestine for the prince of wicked spirits, or demons. Just as, in the language and semiology of the age in which the Gospels were written, God has angels—personal immaterial beings who accomplish his will—so the personified figure of evil has his own angels, who are bitterly hostile to God's creation and humankind, fighting against it with cunning, lies, and deceit.

17.1.2   In the text of the Gospels, there is no reference to the cause, origin, or provenance of the personified figure of evil, nor to an inherited universal dominion of sin over the human race. The most probable reason for this is that the Gospels, records of the kerygma of the first ecclesial communities, borrow and use the language current and understandable by all in their epoch—a language shaped by the metaphysical inquiries and experiences of many generations in the regions of the Near East, and inevitably mingled with elements of instinctive religious attitudes. The aim of the Gospel texts (clearly evident even on a superficial reading) is not to devise an interpretation of evil consistent with the demands of systematic thought but to proclaim a mode (understandable by all) of salvation from evil.

17.2 We encounter an interpretation of the origin, or provenance, of evil (and also of its dominance over the whole of cosmic reality) as current, self-evident, and commonly accepted ideas for the first time in the Epistles of the Apostle Paul. The new elements (that is, elements absent from the Gospels) introduced into Paul's written kerygma are examined in what follows.

17.2.1   The Apostle Paul treats as a historical fact—a fact that belongs to a specific time—the iconic and symbolic Old Testament account of the original, or protoplast, couple (Adam and Eve), from whom the whole human race descends.

17.2.2   He also accepts as a historical fact the "fall" of the first human couple into sin. He identifies *sin* with transgression against a specific divine commandment. God punishes the protoplasts, the first human couple, for the transgression; their punishment is toil for survival, pain in childbirth, and death. When the event of the fall occurs, the protoplast couple constitute the entire human species, and for that reason their punishment affects the whole of humanity diachronically: the penalty is transferred by inheritance to the descendants of the protoplasts. Consequently, by the transgression, or sin, of the first human beings, evil (toil, pain, and death) enters into the world, which God had created as "very good."[5]

17.2.3 Paul accepts a relative mitigation of the responsibility of the protoplasts by also taking as a given from the narrative in Genesis the transgression of the serpent (the personified figure of evil), which deceived humankind with guile.[6] The serpent-devil preexisted humankind, but Paul does not explain *how* and *why* he preexisted or *how* and *why* he had access to "paradise," the place or mode of the first untroubled relationship between humanity and God. Paul does not explain (even though the question had been raised by the Gnosticism of his time) *why* the causal principle of evil should be precosmic or why evil had been given the opportunity to intrude (as a serpent) into God's "very good" creation, enticing humanity to transgress against the divine commandment.

17.2.4 Within the same perspective of historicizing the symbolic narrative of Genesis, Paul divides the history of the human race, as well as the whole of cosmic reality, into two periods: prelapsarian and postlapsarian. Evil (toil, pain, and death) is absent from the prelapsarian period; both the world and humanity embody the "very good" character of the divine creation. In the postlapsarian period, however, not only is humanity now mortal, but "the whole creation has been groaning in labor pains," "subjected to futility" and in "bondage to decay."[7]

   This division of cosmic time into two different and opposing periods, as formulated by Paul, stimulated later Christian hermeneutics to create an imaginary picture of the world in its prelapsarian state based on the idea that until human sin arose, the whole of cosmic reality knew nothing of sin and death. All the animals were herbivores: lions, leopards, and vultures ate nothing but plants and were not subject to death. Roses were without thorns; the land was free of *acanthus* and *brambles*.[8] Human beings were different, too, chiefly in their lack of sexual functions; their reproduction took place by another (unknown) means of *angelic contrivance*.[9]

17.2.5 Paul introduced as a hermeneutic key an understanding of the Church's gospel according to the terms and concepts of legal-juridical experience: he characterizes the sin of the first human beings as *transgression, disobedience*, and *impiety* that provoked the *wrath* of God.[10] God is presented as a loving father, but also as a judge meting out punishments, a judge who "will repay according to each one's deeds," as we know from the past, when "every transgression or disobedience received a just penalty."[11] According to this thinking, the transgression of God's commandment by the first couple implicated the human species as a whole in the guilt—which is transmitted by inheritance as an existential distortion, as "another law that dwells in my members."[12] Moreover, human guilt was transmitted to the entire material creation, distorting the working of cosmic reality as a whole.[13]

17.2.6   The Apostle Paul's interpretation of the reality of evil—evil as the outcome of the disobedience of the first human beings, as guilt that weighs on humanity as a whole and is transmitted by inheritance in spite of the free will and judgment that are supposed to grace humanity—is, of all the ideas peculiar to Paul, the one with perhaps the most serious consequences for the life and teaching of the Church. This is probably a result of its simplistic schematic structure, which lends itself to exploitation by the instinctive urges of natural religiosity.

The fact is that as a consequence chiefly of Paul's theses, Christianity was identified historically in the popular consciousness as a religion of guilt and anxiety. For twenty centuries, billions of people have lived with their one unique life blighted by the fear of judgment for a sin they did not commit but the *condemnation* for which they have inexorably inherited.

17.2.7   The idea of an inherited guilt, transmitted as a result of ancestral sin, also implies, in Paul's perspective, a certain ontological interpretation (referring to the mode of existence) of the relationship between the individual and nature: one human being can alter all humanity's mode of existence and even that of the created order's entire nature. Because of this ontological dimension, in the Pauline perspective, Adam's disobedience had consequences for the whole universe, and similarly, the obedience of Christ to the will of the Father had consequences for the salvation of the universe.[14]

This ontological hermeneutic has no support either in experience or in rational thought (see 16.4.4 above). Moreover, from this perspective, the salvation in Christ of humanity and the world—the core of the Christian gospel—is tied to the historicity of the person of Adam and his disobedience. Thus if Adam is taken only as a symbolic image, a difficult linguistic problem arises for the interpretation and understanding of the Church's witness.

17.3   The difference between the Gospels and Paul's Epistles with regard to the provenance and transmission of evil is not a matter that has occupied Christian thought. Until the natural sciences arose and established their own assertions, the prevailing worldview did not come into conflict with the worldview presupposed by the Bible. One way or another, every traditional cosmogony was mythological, and its hermeneutic proposition had to be extrapolated from its symbolic forms of expression.

17.3.1   Both the language of the Gospels and the language of Paul are examples of a topical code of communication set within the framework of a historically determined cultural paradigm. Both sets of texts presuppose the "reputable opinions" (*endoxa*) of their age; they possess the relativity that is always characteristic of human language.

17.3.2   Both the language of the Gospels and the language of Paul define the experience of the Church, but they do not substitute it. That is why I preceded this section with a discussion of the difference between the *Church* and *natural religion*: so that it would now be clear that the relativity of biblical language does not also relativize the reality of the Church's experience. On the contrary, the idolizing of biblical language replaces and invalidates the Church's experience.

17.4   The picture and understanding we have today of the physical universe does not coincide with the biblical one. The points of difference are stated in summary form in what follows.

17.4.1   There is not the slightest scientific evidence to allow us to suppose that there was an initial phase, period, or evolutionary stage of the natural reality that bears any resemblance or analogy to the so-called prelapsarian state of the world. The findings to date of the natural sciences confirm that the universe, from the first moment of its existence to the present day, has been constituted by the same elements and has been subject to the same physiochemical behavior of the elements, the same stable patterns, the same functional laws, the same thermodynamic axioms, and so forth. The possibility that the world was once material but incorruptible and that with the fall of humanity it became material and corruptible (as certain ecclesiastical writers suppose[15]) has had no scientific support to date.

17.4.2 Millions of years before the appearance of humankind, the phenomenon of life on earth was governed by the same laws that prevail today concerning birth, development, reproduction, decay and death, the progressive evolution of more complex species, the complementary process of mutual destruction, the instincts of self-preservation and pleasure, the many-faceted manifestations of sexuality. The possibility that "death entered into the world through one man," or that sexuality is a consequence of the fall of humanity, or that toil, decay, pain, and pleasure are also products of human disobedience to God's commandments, corresponds to nothing verifiable in the reality of our known physical universe.

17.4.3 In the first centuries of the Church's historical life, and especially in the region of Palestine, oral tradition must have preserved genealogies that located God's creation of humanity in a specific past time. Two such genealogies have been recorded in the Gospels: one by Matthew (starting from Abraham) and one by Luke (going all the way back to Adam).[16] Matthew's list includes forty-two generations, and Luke's, seventy-four. We usually reckon a generation to be twenty-five years, so in the first case Abraham must be dated to about 1050 BC (2,050 years ago), and in the second case the creation of Adam must be assigned to about 1850 BC (3,850 years ago). Modern geology, paleontology, and genetics date the first appearance of the human species as we know it today (*Homo sapiens sapiens*) to about 40,000 years ago.[17]

17.4.4 Given the findings of scientific research that constitute our modern picture and understanding of physical reality, it is difficult to accept the sudden appearance of humankind as a fully formed rational subject. Considering that the human species as we know it today (*Homo sapiens sapiens*) differs in every part of its skeleton even from the archaic *Homo sapiens*, the nearest branch of anthropoids resembling modern humans,[18] the perfection of the capacities for speech and for the formation of a linguistic code, the development of intellectual and critical functions, the ability to use tools, the fostering of a creative imagination, and so forth, must have required a long evolutionary process. At which point in this very slow (by the standard of the individual life) process we can justifiably place Adam, if we consider him a historical person, is a question which clearly falls outside the boundaries of research.[19]

17.5   Toil, pain, agony, fear, torment, sickness, decay, and finally death are real givens in human life, manifestations of the reality interwoven with existence that we human beings call *evil*. The advance of scientific knowledge permits assertions with a satisfactory degree of precision relating to the identification, description, and causal attribution of the symptoms of evil. The question of evil's original point of departure—its causal principle—like the question of the causal principle of the world, falls outside the province of science.

17.5.1   This point bears repeating: science is the knowledge of natural reality that is subject to common verification using methods that are demonstrably reliable. Any proposition identifying the cause and purpose of natural reality (or of those of its manifestations that we human beings call *evil*) is not subject to common verification with methods that are demonstrably reliable (e.g., observation, experiment, mathematical analysis). Consequently, no such proposition can have a scientific character.

17.5.2   Any reply to the question of the cause and purpose—or the *meaning*—of evil, just like any reply to the question of the meaning of the world, has by definition a metaphysical character. The reply is shaped by the terms of common logic, the terms of language and mutual comprehension, and is understood according to these terms. It comes to be accepted or rejected, however—that is, it persuades or does not persuade—according to terms that are much broader and that relate to the empirical assumptions of every human being, to each one's education, sensitivities and ambitions, to the social influences that have affected a person, and to the cultural environment in which one happens to have been born and in which one happens to live—terms that relate to different geographical and historical factors.

17.5.3   Every person arrives or does not arrive at the meaning of the world and the meaning of evil—only never with certainty, never with absolute assurance (unless he alienates the *meaning* and turns it into an *ideology* for individualistic psychological consumption). Every person empirically besieges what he seeks in a unique, dissimilar, and unrepeatable way—or abandons the struggle. It is exactly the same with love and with beauty. If a "scientifically correct" answer existed to the problem of evil, or if there were a "scientifically correct" way for a person to fall in love or to admire beauty, then the human rational subject would not be that which we know it to be.

Hypostatic Rationality and Ontic Indeterminacy

18 For twenty whole centuries, Christian thought interpreted the reality of evil and its original starting point using the iconological language of the Old Testament. This language was sometimes taken in a symbolic or metaphorical sense, sometimes as a description of historical events. At any rate, in all these centuries, the Church's interpretation of the origin of evil was on the whole not disputed by any of the successive pragmatist or scientific worldviews.

Today, opposition to the Church's interpretation is a given supported by abundant evidence—it cannot be ignored.

18.1   The reality of evil has not changed, nor in most cases has the Church's perspective—in spite of the fact that on a quantitative scale the changes that have occurred have been overwhelmingly destructive to that perspective. Yet the language that theological literature uses to interpret evil presupposes an understanding of natural reality that is out of step with today's empirical worldview, as shaped by the inferences of the natural sciences.

The question is this: are there margins that allow the theological language of the interpretation of evil to be coordinated with the findings of modern science? Is it possible for a language to exist that can continue to express the pragmatism of the Church's experience through the ages without coming into conflict with the "reputable opinions" of today's scientific worldview?

18.1.1 The shaping of a (new) language of this kind certainly demands critical thinking over a considerable period that cannot possibly be predetermined. At all events, such a language (1) will inevitably need to distinguish the proposed ontological interpretation from the underlying scientific information, which is always subject to falsification; (2) will not confuse the fields of ontological interpretation and scientific assertion, but neither will it set them in opposition to each other; and (3) will preserve access to that empirical knowledge deriving from the immediacy of relation (as faith or trust), without slipping into *a priori* or dogmatic attitudes—a knowledge equally free from an exclusively intellectual approach on the one hand and the promptings of psychological need on the other.

18.2   On our way to forming a theological interpretation of evil more in conformity with the modern worldview, we can perhaps orient ourselves by drawing on important markers of experience such as the following, which I offer by way of example.

18.2.1 The radically new element that the historical experience of the Church has conveyed to us, and which justifies the term *revelation*, is the *triadic* nature of the causal principle of that which exists.

   If the causal principle of that which exists is *triadic*, then the *mode* of that which really, *in truth*, exists—the *ontōs on*, or "really real"—is also to be located within the *cause* of the existential fact, as the standard or criterion for distinguishing existential authenticity from existential alienation, that is, *good* from *evil*. And this mode, standard, or criterion is *relation*; it is not atomic onticity. Existence is constituted not by its character as a monad of the existential fact (as onticity in itself); it is constituted by relation as *love*—that is, as freedom from any predetermination or other necessity.

   In the field of ontological semantics, the names *Father, Son* or *Logos* of the Father, and *Spirit* of the Father constitute a definition of a mode of existence free from the restrictions and predeterminations of a given *logos* (i.e., of a given essence or nature), of the *logos* of a definite monad (i.e., of essence or nature as a whole), or of a definite individual entity. The cause of the existential fact and the *logos*-mode of real existence is not a particular and definite entity in terms of self-contained individuality but, rather, an existential self-consciousness in terms of the freedom of the entity's self-transcendence within the dynamic of a loving relation.

18.2.2 Within this ontological perspective, there exists a fundamental and defining difference between *uncreated* and *created*. What is uncreated is the triadic oneness of self-existent freedom; what is created is the fruit of this loving existential mode in its "ad extra" realization and manifestation. As the fruit of a causal conception, will, or energy, the created possesses the predeterminations and limitations of a given *logos*—that is, of a given essence or nature—and consequently, as a mode of existence, it also possesses the *logos* that defines atomic onticity.

18.2.3 Human experience recognizes that the mode of existence of the created has limitations not only of a predetermined *eidetic logos* (of essence or nature) but also of a predetermined defining *logos* (of temporality, spatial location, specific margins of activity). The existential limitations of the created have been regarded by human thought as a disadvantage, an existential shortcoming, an impairment of existential possibilities, or a fall, in comparison with the unlimited existential possibilities of the uncreated—possibilities which we infer, however, by a syllogistic process, having the existential limitations of the created as the empirical basis of our anagogic syllogisms.

The unlimited character of the existential possibilities of the uncreated is understood by us more easily as a quantitative (ad infinitum) expansion of the known measures and boundaries of the created—it is more difficult for us to conceive of it as a qualitative dimension of freedom.

18.2.4 It is not only by reasoning anagogically from relative dimensions to absolute dimensions that we conceive of whatever is indicated by reference to *existential freedom from the limitations of time, space, and activity*. It is also possible for empirical, or extremely realistic, starting points for awareness of existential freedom to operate—starting points such as (1) the experience of

the *modally infinite* and the *private absolute*,[1] (2) the experience
of active, not only formal, existential *otherness* (i.e., of poetic and
creative activity, or energy), and (3) the experience of *beauty* as a
summons to a relational otherness (i.e., to an experience of the
epistemic dynamic of erotic love).

18.2.5   If the existential freedom of the uncreated is an articulation
of its mode of existence, if the mode of existence of the uncreated is
loving relationship, not atomic onticity, and if the created rational
subject (humanity) *is born* not by its conception and formation as
a biological atomic entity, but by its entry into the fact of relation
("is born in the space of the Other"), then that result has logical
space: biological death, as the dissolution of atomic onticity, can
be the dissolution of one mode of existence without also annulling
the subject of the mode, the hypostatic presupposition of ecstatic
reference.

     The death of the created human entity, an entity capable of the
reciprocity of relation, could rationally be taken as a positive step
toward some kind of assimilation (*mutatis mutandis*) to the mode
of the freedom of the uncreated.

18.2.6   If the rational subject "is born in the space of the Other,"
then the inference is reasonable that the rational subject dies only
if its existential reference to the "Other" is dissolved. This inference
coincides with the conviction of the Judeo-Christian witness that
death in reality is not the biological death of the human being as an
atomic entity; it is the rupture, or rejection, of the human being's
relation with God.[2]

18.3   Death is included in evil so long as it constitutes a threat to
existence. The natural existence of the rational subject, its biological atomicity, is dissolved by death—nature "knows," by its instinctive "logic," that the ultimate evil for it is death. Fear, dread, or panic
in the face of death, the death agony, is a response that is biological,
instinctive, and reflexive. This response is characteristic of all animate beings—at least, of all that have a developed sensory-nervous
system.

     Dread in the face of death is analogous to hunger, thirst, and
sexual need. Because of hunger, thirst, and sexual need, because

of dread in the face of death, nature survives even though the individual form is ephemeral. The fear of death is not a property of the rational subject; it is not a product of rationality or of the consciousness of one who is aware of the end. It is a function of irrational nature, a necessity for self-preservation.

18.3.1   The propositions of the philosophical schools or religious traditions locate the difference between rational human beings and irrational animals in whatever margins of freedom from the necessities of nature characterize humanity—freedom with regard to the imperatives of hunger, thirst, the sex drive, and the fear of death.[3] The human rational subject operates existentially as a being limited with regard to time, space, and the dynamics of its activities as an individual natural entity. The result of its activities, however, endures as a *logos* of existential otherness, or uniqueness, without limitations of time and space (e.g., the philosophical statements of Heraclitus, the paintings of Panselinos, the music of Bach). Every rational subject, for the duration of its limited natural existence, has an immediacy of relationship with the results of the rational activity of other subjects, independently of time and distance, thus forming a catholic overview of cosmic and historical becoming, a rational overview that is unlimited in comparison with its limited, atomic, natural onticity.

18.3.2   The human subject is *rational* inasmuch as, with the energies or potentialities of its existentially limited, atomic, natural onticity, it realizes a leap of ecstatic existential reference, a leap of effecting or provoking relations free from time and space. Given the conviction that the rational subject also has its fundamental starting point in the fact of relation, there, too, the rational subject is constituted as a hypostatic self-consciousness.

18.3.3   How should we conceive of the subject of existential referential ecstasy as a hypostatic reality not exhausted in natural atomic onticity? By which categories (capable of empirical confirmation) can we signify the hypostatic fact of subjectivity as *activated* by means of brain functions but *realized existentially* as an unlimited fact of relation? The question permits the quandary whether death—the supreme manifestation of evil for natural atomic onticity—also dissolves the hypostatic rationality, which is not subject to definite localization.

18.3.4 In our linguistic usage, we have definite localizations of uniqueness, localizations that do not necessarily refer to a signified ontic atomicity. A characteristic example is the *unconscious*. It comprises urges and fantasies representative of unfulfilled desires, indelible episodes repressed by the conscious mind, or infant experiences which have never been brought to consciousness.[4] And this "deposit," *structured as a language*[5]—as it shows when it fleetingly breaks the surface in, for example, unintended words, clumsy gestures, hesitations, exclamations, and chiefly dreams—constitutes "the other half" of our conscious self: it functions as something homologous, at every point, with that which happens at the surface of the conscious mind.[6]

Thus the reality of the unconscious fatally undermines the Cartesian or definite self-confirmation of the subject as a thinking atomic entity—the self-confirmation of existence by the individual capacity for rational thought. Before the defining certainty of *cogito*, there exists the (presubjective) syntactic structure of language, a structure that constitutes both conscious thought and the working of the unconscious: that is, it confirms a radically primordial *referentiality* as a unique "definition" of the subject—and only *logos* (*le dire, la parole*) is the witness to this confirmation.[7]

The ontic indeterminacy introduced as a "definition" of the subject by the fleeting surfacings of the unconscious does not cease to "isolate within the subject a core (a *Kern*, to use Freud's term) of *non-meaning*"[8]—or of something which transcends any meaning, being the hypostatic potentiality of meaning (i.e., the hypostatic potentiality of the reference, term, and factor of relation).

But even this nucleus must not be taken as an *ontic* definition of the subject; therefore it is characterized as *nonsense*, not because it is really nonexistent but because it is approached only by being manifested—that is, by being referred to, witnessed to by the *logos*. The *logos* constitutes the subject as an existential fact both on the level of consciousness and on the level of the unconscious.[9]

Is Evil an Expression of Rationality, or Freedom?

19 Even if an experiential probing of the subject's ontic indeterminacy allows us to regard an optimistic assessment of physical death as having some degree of probability, the multifaceted reality of evil continues to dominate human life—a universal given but an enigmatic one. The tormenting of one human being by another, crime, violence, enmity, envy, slander, lies, injustice, oppression and the arbitrary exercise of authority, terror and anxiety, sickness and pain, physical decay, destitution, famine—these are among the more frequent manifestations of evil in our daily life.

It is as if something has gone wrong with the human species on planet Earth, as if there has intervened some tragic turning away from the intended goal,

some huge disaster,
some monstrous mistake and aberration.[1]

Even if we were to decide to abandon the search for a causal principle and purpose of that which exists—the search for a benevolent providence for the world—the reality of evil, as experienced by rational human beings, appears incompatible even with the most mechanistic version of the laws and necessities of survival, natural selection, and the perpetuation of the human species. Evil is not a consequence of the relentless character of the laws that govern our natural onticity; universal human experience attributes it primarily to humanity's responsibility for self-preservation. *Homo homini lupus.*

It is therefore no coincidence that almost all cultures have recourse to a supposed fall of humanity from an original level of existence, which was more integrated and more happy, to another level—manifestly inferior, defective, and more miserable.[2]

19.1   We have seen the hermeneutic gaps that an etiological account of evil leaves if we resort to the hypothesis of an original "missing of the mark" (*astochia*), or existential failure, transmitted by inheritance to the whole human race from one supposed original couple. The hermeneutic gaps are not covered even if we transfer responsibility for the putative fall to a rupture with the Creator preceding humanity's failure and perpetrated by some other entity of a spiritual kind, endowed with the marks of rational being (i.e., Satan, or the devil) that also drew humanity into the fall.

19.2   It remains for us to examine whether there is logical space for an interpretation that would derive the existential reality of evil from humanity's *rationality*, that is, from its *freedom*, which is inevitably relative but nevertheless really operative.

19.2.1   We define *rationality* as the referentiality of the primordial desire as determined by language (*le dire, la parole*). We identify it with the power to realize relation.

We distinguish a rational relation from phenomenological or noumenal correlations as well as from any *necessary* connection, coupling, or mutual dependence. *Relation* is the result of rationality, the potentiality for the goal of the primordial desire, libido, to be realized or not attained.

Rational relation is a potentiality because it presupposes the referentiality of desire and the reciprocity of the referential readiness of the terms or factors of the relation (which can be persons or persons plus things, or personal acts[3]).The reference constitutes a *logos* (of desire) and recognizes—that is, encounters—in the object of desire a rational response, positive or negative. All things are possible; nothing in a rational relation is determined by necessities. The rationality lends to the relation the character of potentiality: the realization or failure of the rational relation is not predetermined.

19.2.2 Between the two extremes—the possibility of realizing and the possibility of failing to realize relation—there is an unlimited range of possibilities of fullness and quality of relation.

19.2.3 We describe existential referentiality—that is, referentiality as existential fact, as mode of existence—can be described as *rational* because it expresses a *logos* of desire. And we recognize that the primordial desire in human beings is rational in the degree to which it is erotic: a desire for fulfilling relation, a desire for life-as-relation.[4]

There is also a nonrational desire: that which is exhausted in a biological need and intentionality that has been made autonomous. It is a passive conformity to the natural individual's drive for self-preservation and urge for pleasure.

19.2.4 Every desire is activated by the biological prescriptions or powers of the natural individual. Without biological need, the power of desire is not activated. The difference emerges incidentally: nonrational desire is fulfilled by the satisfaction of natural need. Rational, or erotic, desire is mediated by the natural need but is not exhausted in the satisfaction of the natural need—it aims *beyond* it. This *beyond*, the *something more* than the biological demand—namely, the desire for a fulfilling *relation*, for *life-as-relation*—is the real starting point for the birth of the rational subject.[5]

19.2.5 Natural need (for food, for duration of life) is presupposed for the power, or the *beyond-the-natural* need, of realizing relation to be activated: a power of transition from the other (of need) to the Other (of vital desire).

This transition constitutes a power, not a necessity. The referentiality of desire may possibly be exhausted in the natural need: it may be a demand for possessing, using, or exercising propriatorial rights over the object of the reference. For relation to be realized, the natural need is presupposed, as is the desire for something more than natural need: for the leap of self-transcending reference.

19.3   Within the epithymetic reference, which constitutes rationality, there exist both the possibility of relation and the possibility
of nonrelation—that is, of the rejection or avoidance of relation.

19.3.1   The desire for life-as-relation (libido) coexists in humanity
along with contrary tendencies: the so-called *ego drive*, the *instinct
of self-preservation*, and the *death wish*.[6] The concentration of the
vital desire in self-transcendent referentiality is as likely as its alienation into a centripetal egotistic demand for the subjection, domination, use, and possession of the objective other (and often the
transformation of the *Other person* into the *other thing*). The possibility of relation is put at risk in the form of a dilemma between
desire for life and *urge for death*. Because of this risk, rationality is
born and exists.

19.3.2   With the givens of human experience, we cannot discon-
nect rationality from the dual possibility: affirmation of, or rejection of, relation. Self-transcending referentiality presupposes that
which it transcends, namely, self-centeredness, or the rejection-
repudiation-avoidance of the possibility of relation.

        The possibility of nonrelation, of rupture—the possibility of
that which we human beings call (at least) *moral evil*—appears to
constitute a presupposition of the existence of the rational subject.

19.3.3   The tormenting of one human being by another, crime,
violence, enmity, envy, slander, lies, injustice, domination, oppression: these are forms, manifestations, or consequences of the rejection of relation, of breaking with or repudiating self-transcending
reference.

        Rejection could perhaps—though it would be a rationalis-
tic, utilitarian logical possibility—be restricted to the avoidance
of relation, to bypassing it, so that it should not be transformed
into aggressiveness, into hatred, into an attempt at the neutraliza-
tion, and, if possible, annihilation or destruction, of the person
opposite us. But the rupture, in all the degrees of its intensity, is
a blind (without rational referentiality) attempt at egotistic self-
assertion that automatically transforms the person opposite into a
threat. An unconscious panic about insecurity, mistaken but tormenting fears, leads to the need for the rupture. And the reflexive

instinctive reaction is the armoring of the self with certainties, which the other, the one opposite us, undermines, even if only by existing—by constituting a possibility of being a comparison with, or diminution of, the absoluteness of the defended ego.

This multifaceted and varied aggressiveness is a need for "self-assertion through the ontological erasure of every other presence . . . The life of the individual consists in the rejection of the other; it is constituted as an attempt to free life [itself] from limitation only through omnipotence."[7]

19.3.4 The hermeneutics, then, of the archetypal myth of the fall could be liberated from attempts to locate it etiologically in history and could function with the dynamic universality of the symbol: we may perhaps see in the iconological narrative of the sacred texts of the Judeo-Christian tradition an early model of the existential adventure of every human being, of his freedom, as presupposed by the uniqueness of the gift of rationality.

In What Circumstances the Signifier *Relational Ontology* Is Literally True

20 What we human beings call *moral evil* (*ēthiko kako*) seems to have as its real starting point not the *ēthos*, the "moral character," of humanity but its *nature*.

We define as *moral evil* the consequences that flow from the rejection or rupture of relation, of the relations of communion with life; *moral evil* is the multifaceted and varied aggressiveness that creates an infinite number of grades in this rejection or rupture. But whatever weight of intentionality or habituation we attribute to the word *ēthos*, it is difficult to locate the real starting point and cause of the rejections or ruptures of relation there. The cause is to be located not in the *ēthos* but in the nature of humanity, in its instinctive urge for self-preservation, its drive to dominate and control.

If these remarks correspond in any coherent way to common experience, then what we call *moral evil* cannot really be separated from the reality of the physical-biological human state, for this is the source of our necessary reflexes of self-defense, our uncontrolled propensities, our nonrational desires for selfish autarchy. The symptoms of rupture, nonrelation, and aggressiveness—in other words, of *moral evil*—are an organic consequence of nature; they are manifestations of so-called *natural evil*.[1]

And if we regard moral evil, the rejection or rupture of relation, as a presupposition of the deliberate self-transcendent reference of its potential character, which constitutes the rationality of the subject, then we must recognize in the reality of natural evil (in the nonrationality, autonomy, and necessity of the urges and instincts) a causal condition of rationality.

20.1   Nevertheless, natural evil for human beings is not only the impersonal laws and necessities of each individual's onticity, each one's instinctive drives, nor is it only the existential deficiencies of the nature of the whole (*to katholou*)—decay, sickness, pain, fear, the finiteness of the natural individual in time and space. What is chiefly evil is the relentless and inexorable existential priority in nature of what belongs to the *whole* (*ta katholou*) over what belongs to the *particular* (*ta kathekaston*), of the *species* over the *individual*—the nonrational "indifference" of nature to the hypostases of the existential fact, to the unique, dissimilar, and unrepeatable *logos* of each individual existence.

It is terrifying how easy it is for the uniqueness and even the active, creative otherness that is hypostasized in the rational human subject to be wiped out. Perhaps only so that some microbiological species of pathogen can survive, a gifted artist or a brilliant scientist comes to die in the prime of youth, at the height of his creative powers; the law of nature has no respect for qualities, nor does it show any awe for the unique. Earthquakes, floods, fires, shipwrecks, pestilence, and famine cause the indiscriminate death of human rational existences on a large scale, in a manner no different from the mass destruction suffered by insects and invertebrates.

This mechanistic, inexorable "becoming" of nature, the monstrous indifference to the hypostatic self-consciousness of nature—to the bearer of the *logos* of nature: the human rational subject—is an uninterpretable reality, a reality not susceptible to any attempt to suggest meaning in elementarily realistic terms.

20.1.1 We mean by the expression *natural evil* the reality of nature as a given threat to human hypostatic otherness, to the individual existence of the human person. Not only is objective natural reality (i.e., the reality that "lies opposite" us) a threat and an evil, but so is the natural onticity of the subject itself. Uninterpretable, and hence enigmatic, the threat of evil bides its time, intertwined with the striking beauty and astonishing wisdom of both the objective and the subjective sides of human nature. It is as if the cause of the world, the Other of vital desire, manifests, by the beauty of nature that invites us to relationship, a manic love for his "image," the rational human being—but at the same time keeps the natural existence of the human being, that precisely which constitutes the *logos* and consciousness of the universe, on a constant knife's edge.

20.1.2 Humanity, both in its objective natural reality and in its individual natural onticity, confirms and experiences the threat of evil as an existential deficiency in its relation with the world. Its relation is organic: it breathes, ingests food, appropriates nature as clothing, tools, material for its artifacts—the human being cannot exist without appropriation of the world. But this appropriation is trapped in decay, in sickness, in pain, in fear, and finally in death. The relation of humanity to the world is biogenetic, not life giving.

What, then, is the *meaning* of this relation, which on the one hand conserves natural existence and the possibility of the leap of rationality but on the other ties natural existence to the constant process of destruction? If the rationality of human beings, which is more or less identical with their freedom from nature, is manifested in their relation with objective nature, and if the possibility of relation peculiar to human beings permits them the risk of either affirming or denying the self-transcendence of referentiality, then an active affirmation would also be permitted to be manifested in a relation with nature that, if not life giving, would at least be not death dealing: it would be permitted to abolish the threat of the annihilation of existence, and this abolition would be accessible to common experiential confirmation—not simply reckoned as a probability or as something hoped for with natural, physical death as an unavoidable given.

A possibility of abolishing death, however, offered to common experiential confirmation would surely operate in a compelling way; it would be transformed into a necessity of conforming with the presuppositions of this abolition. It would dissolve the freedom of the risk of self-transcendence—that is to say, the rationality of human beings.

20.2   If the rational subject is born in the space of the Other, then rationality is a birth in the distance separating us from the Other. We experience this distance as a live-giving desire for its transcendence; we experience it as an existential defect, as a "fall" that traps us in the law of death. But thanks to this distance, or fall, the instinct for survival—an instinct that governs created being as a necessity—is constituted as a desire for *life-as-relation*, as an active (relatively free) management of self-transcending referentiality.

20.2.1 Thus the fall is revealed to be identical with createdness, but without createdness being diminished or devalued—the fall is not attributed to the material or caused character of created beings. When I speak of the fall, I do not mean some temporal (i.e., occurring in historical time) transition from a higher to a lower level of existence; I do not mean a localized alienation but a comparative difference, a difference of *distance* from the fullness of life-as-relation. I compare our created existence, our experience of its ties and limitations, with the experience of the primordial desire that constitutes us as rational subjects—I compare createdness with the goal of the desire: life-as-relation, "life which is immortal, life which is irrepressible, life which has no need of any organ, life which is simplified and indestructible."[2]

(A useful linguistic signifier enabling the *space* of the "Other" to be manifested, the *space* of the primordial—and final—longed-for self-transcending referentiality of our existence, is the designation of the cause-in-itself and life-in-itself as a *triad of personal hypostases*. This linguistic signifier is indicative of ontic self-transcendence and loving mutual indwelling as existential fullness. "Monad unoriginate and simple, the same both monad and triad; the same wholly monad and the same wholly triad . . . monad unconfused and triad undivided . . . the same wholly monad according to essence and the same wholly triad according to the hypostases."[3] This is a linguistic formulation rich with meaning.)

20.2.2 If the fall, as distance from existential fullness, is birth into rationality, the cause of "the knowledge of good and evil,"[4] this constitutes the specific difference of humanity from every other created existence, because thanks to this fall or distance, the desire can be life giving: desire for existence as relation. And if existential referentiality can be self-transcendent, humanity can exist and be free of the necessities of its created nature. It can exist not exclusively by the mode of createdness but also by the mode of relative likeness to—in the image of—the uncreated.

20.2.3 This hermeneutic perspective perhaps frees our understanding of the fall from the need for a legal framework or from doubtful attempts to fit it into a historical context. But of course, it does not solve the problem of evil; it does not suggest a cause for the undermining of the hypostasis of the existential fact that is inherent in nature, the sadistic exploitation that nature holds in store for the human rational subject.

At any rate, if in the mode of *relation*, of loving self-transcendence, we approach (with the relativity of language always in mind) the "space of the Other"—the goal of the life-giving desire, the goal of freedom from the limitations of createdness—then the natural death of ontic atomicity can be interpreted as a breaking down of the barrier that separates created nature from the existential freedom of a rational ("personal") hypostasis. The epistemic approach of such an eventuality, however, must not be subject to the limitations of understanding by comparison, by the "objectivity" that is presupposed by language. The epistemic approach should be accessible in the degree and manner in which certain experiential probings become accessible in the fields of love and art, as a result of the struggle for self-denial made by the lover or the artist.

20.2.4 We know nothing about any possible existence of the rational after death. We have no possibility of an objective (linguistic) approach to such an eventuality. The limits of the semantic powers of our language are the limits of our experience in this world—or perhaps also the hypothetical and imaginary inferences we draw from this experience. The "certainties" that every manifestation of natural religion conveys about a continuation of human existence after death demand, rather, to be interpreted as a syndrome consistent with the instinctive need for self-preservation.

Only by the path of experiential probing, like that which is achieved in the fields of love and art—the self-denial of the lover or the artist—only by this path can the insistence of the Judeo-Christian tradition on the identification of death not with the destruction of physical individuality but with the rupture of the relation between humanity and God function as a pointer.

20.2.5 The conclusion, at any rate, of clinical observation that the "rational subject is born in the space of the Other"[5] seems to be compatible with the Judeo-Christian suggestion: if the *birth* of the rational subject is not the result of biological necessity, why should its death be so? Why should the *death* of the rational subject not be the denial or rejection (not bound to biological necessity) of the life-giving reference of desire to the Other, of *relation* with the Other?

20.2.6 "*Desidero* is the Freudian *cogito*"[6]—before thought, desire is a relation that constitutes subjectivity and makes it rational. Both desire and rationality are mediated by humanity's energies, or powers, by functions that belong chiefly to the brain. When the mediation ceases with physical death, does that which has been mediated continue to constitute an existential fact? Can the qualitative difference between the impersonal (nonrational) *urge* and the personal (eliciting *logos*) *desire*, or between *perception* and *self-conscious rationality*, be identified as an existential fact not subject to biological necessity?

20.3   It is more than clear that the attempt to shed hermeneutic light on the *beginning* and the *end* of our individual rational existence, an attempt to discover whether it is *finite* or *infinite*, exceeds the competence of the methods and means that (up to now, at least) we have at our disposal.

20.3.1 The knowledge that we can have, both of the sensible reality of the world and of the qualitative differences of our rational self-conscious existence, is an articulation both of the epistemic powers of our human nature and of their subjective (in every separate individual) expression. Our knowledge of the world and of ourselves is relative—the information that our senses convey to us is relative,[7] the powers of our brain functions are relative. We cannot transcend the boundaries of our epistemic powers, nor can we compare our own boundaries even with merely the perception of reality that other animate beings have.

20.3.2 The reference to the impossibility of our comparing and evaluating our perception of the real with the perception, say, that a dolphin or a bat has, is intended also to emphasize, beyond the relativity, the specific prescriptions or factors that set limits to our perception and to whatever knowledge we succeed in attaining. For example, we always conceive of the really existent according to factors of *cause* and *purpose*, *space* and *time*, *beginning* and *end*, *part* and *whole*. By our imagination or our intuition, we transcend these *a priori* factors, but the transcending is realized, rather, in contradistinction to what is defined (identified) by these very factors.

20.3.3 In what we have defined here as a fact of relation and a mode of relation, we are trying to trace possible capacities for knowledge before even those which govern our perception of reality.

In the fact of relation and in the mode of relation—of the ecstatic[8] (from natural drives) reference—we discern the presupposition of every manifestation of human rationality, of every perceptive or epistemic function, of every epistemic experience of beauty, of erotic self-transcendence, of anagogic ascent to otherness, of semantic demonstrations of otherness, of sharing in semantic demonstrations.

20.3.4 If relation is a real presupposition of existence and knowledge for humanity (the mode by which we exist and know), then the factors—essential for perception to function—of *cause* and *purpose*, *space* and *time*, *beginning* and *end*, although constituted as experiential givens by *relation*, are only the horizon of every fact of relation, boundary markers or measures of the fact of relation.[9] And, as measures or boundary markers, they inevitably have some character of objectivity—that is, they cannot be taken as subjective products of rational referentiality; they have at least the "objectivity" of language.

So when we signify the "Other" of our ecstatic reference as the causal principle and purpose and wholeness (fullness) of the rationality of the human subject, these signifiers refer primarily to the experience of a fact of relation, a fact that is marked or measured by the signifiers. Consequently, although our semantics presupposes an experiential epistemic power, it does not impose it as a certainty of mere understanding.

20.3.5 The question whether the "Other" of our existential reference is the real (empirically accessible) second term of the fact of relation—and not a projection of desire or a compensation for insecurity—is a question of verification constructed exclusively by the dynamics of relation. That is why faith, or trust, in God—who exercises providence, who is the giver of good things, the irradiator of sensible reality, the "bridegroom" and "most manic lover" of every human being—is always a personal adventure of verification without any *a priori* guarantee of certainty.

20.4   The Christian presence in human history conveys an aphoristic assurance of dramatic relevance: "And even the hairs of your head are all counted."[10] This is verified strikingly by the dazzling wisdom and beauty of the world, and falsified painfully by the reality of the evil that dominates the world. The phrase summarizes the only adequate meaning we can give to the existence of the world and of humanity. If this phrase is true, all things have meaning. If it is not true, then the existential fact is only an aberration, a macabre farce, an inexplicable riddle.

20.4.1 This aphoristic assurance will be constantly verified and constantly falsified. If the verification or falsification could have been confirmed definitively, it would have presupposed or constituted the abolition of human rationality, of the existential fact of human freedom. Why this rationality, or freedom, should be a permanent issue at the cutting edge of knowledge and ignorance is also a question that perhaps finds a reply only in the field of experiential soundings, such as those achieved by the self-denial of the lover or the artist.

20.4.2 Of course, there are indicators that help, indicators that are not under the discipline of the objectifying function of language without ceasing to refer to a possibly epistemic probing (always with alertness to the distinction between the real and the imaginary, between communicated—in whatever sense—experience and individual delusion).

20.5   The possibility that the rational individual should not be subject to the law of biological death can be traced only through uncertain indications, indirect epistemic probing—as "in a mirror, dimly."[11] These uncertain indications or indirect probing constitute a proposition of the *meaning* of existence and of that which exists. They amount to a thematic analysis of the signifier *relational ontology*.

Notes

Chapter 1

1. *Definitive* (*oristikos*) is: that which belongs to or refers to the definition, that which defines a person or thing in such a way that it distinguishes it from other similar persons or things. (See the entries under *oristikos* in Dimitrakos's and Babiniotis's Greek dictionaries.)

2. See Christos Yannaras, *Meta-neōterikē meta-physikē* (Athens: Domos, 1993), 189, translated by Norman Russell as *Postmodern Metaphysics* (Brookline, MA: Holy Cross Orthodox Press, 2004), 135.

3. For the etymological derivation of *relation* (*schesis*) and a fuller discussion of the concept it signifies, see Christos Yannaras, *To rhēto kai to arrhēto: Ta glōssika oria realismou tēs metaphysikēs* (Athens: Ikaros, 1999), 31ff.; Yannaras, *Protaseis kritikēs ontologias*, 3rd ed. (Athens: Domos, 1995), §§ 1.2, 1.32, 1.331, 1.332, 2.1, 2.11, 2.331; Yannaras, *Meta-neōterikē meta-physikē*, 137ff., 162ff., 189ff.; Yannaras, *Postmodern Metaphysics*, 91ff., 112ff., 135ff.

Chapter 2

1. See the select bibliography in Christos Yannaras, *Orthos logos kai koinōnikē praktikē*, 2nd ed. (Athens: Domos, 1990). See also Yannaras, *Schediasma Eisagōgēs stē Philosophia*, 4th ed. (Athens: Domos, 1994) and its French translation, *Philosophie sans rupture* (Geneva: Labor et Fides, 1998); and Yannaras, *Heidegger kai Areopagitēs*, 4th ed. (Athens: Domos, 1998) and its English translation, *On the Absence and Unknowability of God: Heidegger and the Areopagite* (London and New York: T&T Clark International, 2005).

2. Aristotle, *Rhetoric* A, 1358a4.

3. Wittgenstein, "Das Mystiche (Unaussprechliches) zeigt sich," *Tractatus logico-philosophicus*, 6.522, trans. D. F. Pears and B. F. Mc-Guinness (London: Routledge, 1974). All quotations from the *Tractatus* are from the Pears-McGuinness translation.

4. See Yannaras, *To rhēto kai to arrhēto*, chaps. 1 and 2.

5. See Wittgenstein, *Tractatus*, 3.324.

6. I draw these linguistic expressions at random from Stelios Ramfos, *O kaēmos tou enos* (Athens: Armos, 2000). Translated by Norman Russell as *Yearning for the One: Chapters in the Inner Life of the Greeks* (Brookline, MA: Holy Cross Orthodox Press, 2011).

7. Heraclitus, *Kath' ho,ti an koinōnēsōmen, alētheuomen; ha de an idiasōmen, pseudometha*, in Diels and Kranz, *Fragmente der Vorsokratiker* (Berlin: Weidmannsche, 1952), 1:148, 29–30.

8. See Yannaras, *Schediasma eisagōgēs stē philosophia*, §§ 13, 14, 15; Yannaras, *Protaseis kritikēs ontologias*, § 2.21; Yannaras, *Orthos logos kai koinōnikē praktikē*, 5.1.a.

9. See Yannaras, *Schediasma eisagōgēs stē philosophia*, §§ 8, 11, 13, 14, 18; Yannaras, *Protaseis kritikēs ontologias*, §§ 2.11, 2.21, 2.36, 2.37; Yannaras, *Orthos logos kai koinonikē praktikē*, 5.1.a; Yannaras, *To pragmatiko kai to phantasiōdes stēn politikē oikonomia*, 2nd ed. (Athens: Domos, 1966), 278–82; Yannaras, *Meta-neōterikē meta-physikē*, 125–44; Yannaras, *Postmodern Metaphysics*, 83–97; Yannaras, *E apanthrōpia tou dikaiōmatos* (Athens: Domos, 1998), 33–34; Yannaras, *To rhēto kai to arrhēto*, 35–40.

Chapter 3

1. 1 John 4:8. All biblical quotations are from the New Revised Standard Version.

2. "Le sujet, *in initio*, commence au lieu de l'Autre . . . Le sujet naît en tant qu'au champ de l'Autre surgit le signifiant" (Jacques Lacan, *Le séminaire de Jacques Lacan*, Livre 11 [Paris: Seuil, 1973], 180, 181).

3. The eucharistic prayer from the Divine Liturgy of St. John Chrysostom.

4. "An accident is that which cannot exist in itself but has its being in another . . . contemplated in the essence . . . like a body and color; for the body is not in the color but the color in the body" (John Damascene, *Dialectica*, ed. Bonifatius Kotter [Berlin: Walter de Gruyter, 1969], 58).

Chapter 4

1. See Jacques Lacan, "Les formations de l'inconscient," in *Bulletin de Psychologie* (1957–58): 1–15. See also Jacques Lacan, "Subversion du

sujet et dialectique du désir dans l'inconscient freudien," in *Écrits* (Paris: Seuil, 1971), 2:151ff.

2. "An anorexic infant *makes* himself die, his psyche is stronger than his biological regulatory system" (Cornelius Castoriadis, *The Imaginary Institution of Society*, trans. Kathleen Blamey [Cambridge, MA: MIT Press, 1998], 289).

3. Jacques Lacan, *Le séminaire* 11:23, 180, 181. In *Orthos logos kai koinōnikē praktikē*, *Postmodern Metaphysics*, and *To rhēto kai to arrhēto*, I have tried to show the horizons that are opened up for anthropological-ontological questions by the above statements (based on clinical observation) of Lacan's. My discussions still await either critical confirmation or refutation.

4. See, for example, the representative statements of the Nobel prize winner Gerald M. Edelman, one of the most distinguished scientists specializing in the brain, especially his *Bright Air, Brilliant Fire: On the Matter of the Mind* (New York: Basic Books, 1992): "No amount of neuroscientific data alone can explain thinking . . . A neuroscientific explanation is necessary but is not sufficient as an ultimate explanation" (174). "Diderot's view of human consciousness opened up the possibility that to be human was to go beyond mere physics" (167). "The theories of modern physics and the findings of neuroscience rule out not only a machine model of the world but also such a model of the brain . . . it is clear that each individual person is like no other and is not a machine" (171). "That it emerges from definite material arrangements in the brain does not mean that it is identical to them" (198). "Human memory is not at all like computer memory . . . In biological systems, memory must not be confused with the mechanisms that are necessary for its establishment, such as synaptic change" (237–38). "Now we begin to see why digital computers are a false analogue to the brain" (225). "We have already shown that formal semantics cannot refer unambiguously to the real state of affairs . . . semantic contents are meaningless without intentionality or the ability to refer to other states or objects" (238).

Chapter 5

1. "C'est par la réalité sexuelle que le signifiant est entré au monde, ce qui veut dire que l'homme a appris à penser" (Lacan, *Le séminaire* 11:138).

2. See J. Laplanche and J.-B. Pontalis, *Vocabulaire de la psychanalyse*, 7th ed. (Paris: Presses universitaires de France, 1981). I have used the Greek translation, *Lexilogio tēs Psychanalysēs* (Athens: Kedros, 1986), 409.

3. *Lexilogio tēs Psychanalysēs*, 262.

4. Ibid., 50.

5. "La libido . . . c'est la présence, effective et comme telle, du désir" (Lacan, *Le séminaire* 11:140).

6. Ibid., 161.

7. Denis Vasse, *Le temps du désir* (Paris: Seuil, 1969), 28–29.

8. "Dans le procès de la réalité psychique" (Lacan, *Le séminaire* 11:160).

9. Ibid., 186.

10. "La pulsion saisissant son objet apprend en quelque sorte que ce n'est justement pas par là qu'elle est satisfaite" (ibid., 153).

Chapter 6

1. For fuller discussions of the naturalistic approach to sexuality, see, for example, the following works: Donald Symons, *The Evolution of Human Sexuality* (New York: Oxford University Press, 1979); Desmond Morris, *Bodywatching: A Field Guide to the Human Species* (London: Book Club Associates, 1986); M. Daly and M. Wilson, *Sex, Evolution and Behavior*, 2nd ed. (Boston: PWS Publishers, 1983); Jared Diamond, *Why is Sex Fun? The Evolution of Human Sexuality* (New York: Harper Collins, 1997); Helen E. Fisher, *The Sex Contract: The Evolution of Human Behavior* (New York: William Morrow, 1983); William G. Eberhard, *Sexual Selection and Animal Genitalia* (Cambridge, MA: Harvard University Press, 1985); F. A. Beach, ed., *Human Sexuality in Four Perspectives* (Baltimore: Johns Hopkins University Press, 1976); R. A. Fisher, *The Genetical Theory of Natural Selection* (New York: Oxford University Press, 1999); G. F. Miller, "Evolution of the Human Brain through Runaway Sexual Selection: The Mind as a Protean Courtship Device" (PhD diss., Psychology Department, Stanford University, 1993); and R. R. Baker and M. A. Bellis, *Human Sperm Competition: Copulation, Masturbation and Infidelity* (London: Chapman and Hall, 1995).

Chapter 7

1. Ludwig Wittgenstein, *Philosophical Grammar*, ed. Rush Rhees, trans. Anthony Kenny (Oxford: Blackwell, 1974), A1, 6.

2. Ray Monk (summarizing Wittgenstein) in his *Ludwig Wittgenstein: The Duty of Genius* (London: Jonathan Cape, 1990), 410.

3. "The problem at once presents itself, in what sense we are to speak of parts of the soul, or how many should we distinguish. For in a sense there is an infinity of parts: it is not enough to distinguish, with some thinkers, the calculative, the passionate, and the desiderative, or with others the rational and the irrational; for if we take the dividing lines

followed by these thinkers we shall find parts far more distinctly separated from one another than these" (Aristotle, *On the Soul* 3, 432a22–28;
Oxford translation).

4. Lacan, *Le séminaire* 11:141.

5. Sigmund Freud, "Die sexuellen Abirrungen," in *Drei Abhandlungen zur Sexualtheorie* (Leipzig: Teschen, 1905).

6. Sigmund Freud, "Formulierungen über die zwei Prinzipien des
psychischen Geschehens," in *Gesammelte Werke*, vol. 8.

7. "Libido . . . die Energie solcher Triebe, welche mit all dem zu tun
haben, was man als Liebe zusammenfassen kann" (Sigmund Freud, "Suggestion und Libido," in *Massenpsychologie und Ich-Analyse* [Leipzig: Internationaler Psychoanalytischer Verlag, 1921]).

8. Sigmund Freud, *Jenseits des Lustprinzips* (Leipzig: Internationaler Psychoanalytischer Verlag, 1920), pt. 6.

9. "So würde also die Libido unserer Sexualtriebe mit dem Eros der
Dichter und Philosophen zusammenfallen, der alles Lebende zusam-
menhält" (ibid).

Chapter 8

1. See, for example: John Searle, *Minds, Brains and Science* (Cambridge, MA: Harvard University Press, 1984), 87–88; W. S. McCulloch,
Embodiments of Mind (Cambridge, MA: MIT Press, 1989), 163ff.; Gordon
M. Shepherd, *Neurobiology* (New York: Oxford University Press, 1983),
201–3; Roger Penrose, *The Large, the Small and the Human Mind* (Cambridge: Cambridge University Press, 1997); J. C. Eccles, *How the Self Controls Its Brain* (Berlin: Springer, 1994).

2. See Albert Einstein, *Mein Weltbild* (Berlin: Ullstein, 1934), 168:
"The highest duty of the physicist is to search for those very general laws
. . . from which by a clear inference we can draw the image of the world.
There is no logical path which can lead to these laws. One can arrive at
them only through an intuition based on something which resembles
an intellectual love [Einfühlung] for the objects of experience." See also
Karl Popper, *Logik der Forschung* (Tübingen: J. C. Mohr, 1982), 7.

3. Edelman, *Bright Air, Brilliant Fire*; Hilary Putnam, *Representation
and Reality* (Cambridge, MA: MIT Press, 1988); Searle, *Minds, Brains
and Science*; Penrose, *The Large, the Small and the Human Mind*; Steven
Pinker, *Language Learnability and Language Development* (Cambridge,
MA: Harvard University Press, 1984); Mark Johnson, *The Body in the
Mind: The Bodily Basis of Meaning, Imagination, and Reason* (Chicago:
University of Chicago Press, 1987); Jacques Lacan, "Les quatre concepts
fondamentaux de la psychanalyse," in *Le séminaire* 11 (Paris: Seuil, 1973).

Chapter 10

1. 1 John 4:9. It should be noted, however, that there cannot be philological certainty that in the semantic context of the specific text the phrase is used in an ontological sense.

2. Aristotle, *On the Soul* 3.4, 429a27–29 and 3.8, 432a2.

3. Aristotle, *Metaphysics* 11.7, 1072b20.

4. Aristotle, *Nicomachean Ethics* 10.7, 1177a16; *On the Soul* 3.5, 430a18 and 1.4, 408b18; *Metaphysics* 1.3, 984b15.

5. Aristotle, *On the Soul* 3.5, 430a13–14 and 15–16.

6. Aristotle, *Metaphysics* 1.3, 984b15–17.

7. Leucippus, *On Mind*, frg. 2.

8. Aristotle, *Metaphysics* 11.7.

9. 1 Cor 1:23.

10. *Self-contained* (*autotelēs*): "That which has its end (*telos*) or goal (*skopos*) in itself, that which is self-sufficient or in itself perfect and complete" (Dimitrakos, *Lexikon tēs Ellēnikēs Glossēs*, 1212).

11. *Autonomous* (*autonomos*): "That which is administered by its own laws, that which lives independently, that which determines its own affairs of its own accord and independently of external influences" (Dimitrakos, *Lexikon*, 1203–4).

12. John 15:26: "When the Advocate comes, whom I will send to you from the Father, the Spirit of truth who proceeds from the Father" (NRSV modified); John 16:7–8: "If I do not go away, the Advocate will not come to you; but if I go, I will send him to you. And when he comes, he will prove the world wrong about sin and righteousness and judgment."

13. For the semiological derivation of the signifiers *logos* and *spirit*, see Yannaras, *Protaseis kritikēs ontologias* (Athens: Domos, 1985), 1.3, 1.31, 1.32, 1.33, 1.331, 1.332, 1.333, 1.34, 1.341, 2.371, 2.372–73, 3, 3.1, 3.11.

Chapter 11

1. Wittgenstein, *Tractatus* 5.6.

2. 1 Cor 13:12.

3. The anaphora of the Divine Liturgy of St. John Chrysostom.

4. Maximus the Confessor, *Scholia on the Divine Names*, Migne, Patrologia Graeca (PG) 4:189b.

5. Ibid., 212a, 245c.

6. Maximus the Confessor, *Mystagogia* (PG 91:664a–c).

7. John Damascene, *On the Orthodox Faith* 1, 13.

8. Dionysius the Areopagite, *Mystical Theology* 5 (PG 4:1045d–1048ad).

9. "When souls are purified, they see not in a bodily way but spiritually . . . And if spiritual natures are absent from each other, they still

see each other, because distances and bodily senses do not hinder them from seeing each other . . . Because bodily vision is manifest it sees what is in front of it, but those things that are distant need another kind of vision" (Isaac the Syrian, *Oration 67*, in *Ascetical Works* [Leipzig, 1770; repr., Athens: Ch. Spanos, n.d.], 265).

Chapter 12

1. In theological language, "the divine economy."
2. Rom 2:14–17.
3. See the section entitled "The experience of the private absolute" (thesis 2.2) in Yannaras, *Postmodern Metaphysics.*
4. Plato, *Symposium* 210e4.
5. Yannaras, *To rhēto kai to arrhēto*, 4.6, 51.
6. The Freudian terms are *Bemächtigungstrieb* ("instinct to master"), *pulsion d'emprise*, and *Sadomasochismus.*

Chapter 14

1. [*To aschēmo* (lit. "the shapeless") is, even today, the Greek word for "ugliness."—Trans.]
2. "This is the fall of the soul, to come in this way to matter and to become weak, because all its powers do not come into action; matter hinders them from coming by occupying the place which soul holds and producing a kind of cramped condition, and making evil what it has got hold of by a sort of theft—until soul manages to escape back to its higher state" (Plotinus, *Enneads* 1.8.14 [Armstrong, LCL]).
3. "What is it, then, which has made the souls forget their father, God, and be ignorant of themselves and him, even though they are parts which come from his higher world and altogether belong to it? The beginning of evil for them was audacity (*tolma*) and coming to birth and the first otherness and the wishing to belong to themselves. Since they were clearly delighted with their own independence, and made great use of self-movement, running the opposite course and getting as far away as possible, they were ignorant even that they themselves came from that world; just as children who are immediately torn from their parents and brought up far away do not know who they themselves or their parents are. Since they do not any more see their father or themselves, they despise themselves through ignorance of their birth and honour other things, admiring everything rather than themselves, and, astonished and delighted by and dependent on these [earthly] things, they broke themselves loose as far as they could in contempt of that from which they turned away" (Plotinus, *Enneads* 5.1.1 [Armstrong, LCL]).

4. This is the title of Basil of Caesarea's *Homily* 9 (PG 31:329–53).

5. "Evil is a privation of good" (Basil of Caesarea, *Homily* 9.4 [PG 31:341b]). "I did not enquire whether evil and good are opposites but about their being. For things that have existence (*ta gar onta*) are not entirely opposites; insofar as they have being itself, they share in each other, for the opposite to being is nonbeing. So if evil is altogether the opposite to good, it is good and is not evil. So evil is a privation of being" (John Damascene, *Against the Manichaeans* 1.13, ed. Kotter, 4:357–58). "Evil, whose being is characterized by nonexistence" (Maximus the Confessor, *Ambigua* [PG 91:1332a]).

6. 1 John 1:1–3.

Chapter 15

1. The Church's reliance on the apophatic character of its formulations also manifests the Hellenic derivation of the historical flesh of the Church's gospel, for *apophaticism* is the fundamental epistemological principle of the ancient Greek mode of expression. Such reliance, moreover, manifests the nonreligious character of Greek metaphysics—the priority given by the Greeks to the struggle to interpret that which exists (the "battle of the giants") over any psychological recourse to an easy acceptance of axioms.

2. See Luke 18:9–14; Matt 19:30; 20:27; 21:31; Luke 15:11–32; Mark 9:35.

3. See Gal 3:10–14; Rom 3:19; 4:15; 7:7; 1 Cor 15:56; Eph 2:15.

Chapter 16

1. Gregory of Nyssa, *On the Inscriptions of the Psalms* (PG 44:441b), trans. by Casimir McCambley as *Commentary on the Inscriptions of the Psalms* (Brookline, MA: Hellenic College Press, n.d.), 29.

2. See Genesis 1:31: "God saw everything that he had made, and indeed, it was very good" (LXX: *kala lian*).

3. See Basil of Caesarea's homily by this title (PG 31:329–53).

4. We call a *biocycle* (biological cycle) the totality of the stages and phases that every vegetal and animal organism goes through—the consistently repeated succession of generation, development, reproduction, decay, and death. We regard the individual biocycle of every animate being as beginning with the fertilized ovum from which it derives and ending with the fertilized ovum of the next generation.

5. We call the *food chain* a relationship of a succession of organisms in which the one preceding constitutes the food of its successor—linked together in the order in which the one constitutes the food of the

other. For example: producer (plant), first consumer (herbivorous animal), second consumer (carnivorous animal), colonizer (microorganism, earthworm, etc). The individual of every animal species survives by causing the death of individuals of other species (flora or fauna) with the aim of nourishment (or, in certain cases, reproduction as well). The same individual will be caused to die at some moment, directly or indirectly, for the preservation of other species (if nothing else, of microbes, bacilli, bacteria, viruses, or colonizers). It is because of death, because of mutual destruction, that life is perpetuated.

6. We call *natural selection* one of the more important consequences of a given food chain: by the process of destroying each other, the biologically weaker individuals are more easily caught, and consequently shorter-lived, whereas the more resistant (stronger) individuals are assured of a longer life and a greater chance to breed. There is thus a natural cull, a *selection* of individuals more apt to serve the dynamics of the evolution of the species. If we broaden our perspective to include the plant world, a fuller definition of *natural selection* would run as follows: individuals of every species, with their genetic differences as givens, also have different probabilities of being represented in succeeding generations.

Chapter 17

1. "He will save his people from their sins" (Matt 1:21); "they were baptized . . . confessing their sins" (Matt 3:6); "you will die in your sin" (John 8:21); "everyone who commits sin is a slave to sin" (John 8:34); "when [the Paraclete] comes, he will prove the world wrong about sin" (John 16:8).

2. "The one who handed me over to you is guilty of a greater sin" (John 19:11); "people will be forgiven for their sins and whatever blasphemies they utter; but whoever blasphemes against the Holy Spirit can never have forgiveness, but is guilty of an eternal sin" (Mark 3:28–29).

3. Matt 18:15.

4. Luke 15:18.

5. "For Adam was formed first, then Eve; and Adam was not deceived, but the woman was deceived" (1 Tim 2:13–14); "death exercised dominion from Adam to Moses" (Rom 5:14); "just as sin came into the world through one man, and death came through sin, and so death spread to all because all have sinned" (Rom 5:12); "because of the one man's trespass, death exercised dominion through that one . . . one man's trespass led to condemnation for all" (Rom 5:17–18).

6. "The serpent deceived Eve by its cunning" (2 Cor 11:3).

7. Rom 8:20–22.

8. "The rose was then without thorns . . . the flower did not bloom for a brief period and then die, but its pleasure endured for ever, delighting the eyes and remaining immortal; its scent never satiated; its color constantly flashed forth. No violent winds troubled it, no new moons withered it, no frosts choked it, no burning of the sun parched it . . . And there was the spectacle of a variety of animals, all tame, all well-disposed to each other and listening and calling to each other attentively. The serpent at that time was not frightening but mild and tame, not a wild creature writhing and creeping face-down on the ground but upright and walking on legs. The rest of the irrational animals were similarly gentle, all those that are now wild and savage" (Gregory of Nyssa, *Homily on Paradise* (of doubtful authenticity), in *Gregorii Nysseni Opera, Supplementum*, ed. Had. Hörner [Leiden: Brill, 1972], 77a, 78a, 79a, 80a]). "The first giving of the law granted the enjoyment of fruit . . . for fruit and vegetables were given to us and to the wild beasts and to the birds of the sky and to all of the animals on earth . . . The leopard . . . and the lion . . . subjected to the law of nature were nourished by fruit. But because humanity began to live luxuriously and went beyond what was laid down for it, after the flood the Lord, knowing that human beings were extravagant, allowed a relaxation for all . . . From that time the lion became a carnivore, from that time, too, the vultures have looked for carrion. For surely the vultures, together with all the animals that have been generated, did not search the land. For there was nothing reproduced or brought into being by God that had died yet so that the vultures should find food . . . There were not yet any dead [animals], not yet any smells of decay, not yet any such food for vultures, but all fed like swans and all things grazed in the meadows" (Pseudo-Gregory of Nyssa, *On Let Us Make Man, Homily* 2 [PG 44:284bc]).

9. "Since [the protoplasts] of God disobeyed . . . they lost . . . the beauty of virginity . . . Since they received corruption as a result of death and the curse and pain and a life of toil, it was then that marriage slipped in with them . . . Do you see where marriage took its origin, why it was thought to be necessary? For where there is death, there too is marriage; if the former does not exist, the latter does not follow . . . What marriage, tell me, gave birth to Adam, what pains gave birth to Eve? . . . Ten thousand myriads of angels serve God and none of these came into being by succession, none of them by birth and pains and conceptions . . . After the disobedience when Adam knew Eve his wife, after the fall from paradise, it was then that sexual intercourse first took place. Before the disobedience they imitated the angelic life and there was no question of sexual intercourse" (John Chrysostom, *On Virginity* [PG 48:544–46], and *Homilies on Genesis* [PG 53:123–24, 153]). "Conception through seed and birth though decay was drawn down upon itself by nature after the

transgression" (Maximus the Confessor, *Ambigua* [PG 91:1341c]). "The man was created male by the Creator . . . for knowing in his foreknowledge that the man would enter into transgression and would fall under the power of corruption, God made the female out of him, 'a helper as his partner,' a helper for the constitution of the race by succession through birth after the transgression. For the first creation is called a generation (*genesis*) and not a birth (*gennēsis*); for a generation is the first creation from God, while birth is the succession from others as a result of the condemnation of death through the transgression" (John Damascene, *On the Orthodox Faith* 44, ed. B. Kotter [Berlin: Walter de Gruyter, 1973], 104, 228). "When death came into the world through the transgression, then 'Adam knew his wife Eve and she conceived and gave birth' . . . because the 'increase and multiply' does not necessarily indicate a multiplication through sexual intercourse. God could have multiplied the race by another means if they had kept the commandment inviolate until the end" (ibid., 228). "Life before the transgression was an angelic one . . . there is no marriage among them [the angels], yet the armies of angels exist in infinite myriads . . . Therefore, even if there had been no falling away and loss of angelic status as a result of sin, we too would have had no need for marriage for us to multiply. But whatever is the mode of increase in the angels' nature, although ineffable and inaccessible to human thought, that would certainly have been the case with human beings" (Gregory of Nyssa, *On the Making of Man*, chap. 17 [PG 44:188–89]).

10. "The wrath of God comes on those who are disobedient" (Eph 5:6); "the spirit that is now at work among those who are disobedient" (Eph 2:2); "you were once disobedient to God" (Rom 11:30); "for the wrath of God is revealed from heaven against all ungodliness" (Rom 1:18); "Christ died for the ungodly" (Rom 5:6); "[grace] training us to renounce impiety . . . to live lives that are . . . godly" (Titus 2:12); "for if while we were enemies, we were reconciled to God through the death of his Son, much more surely, having been reconciled, will we be saved by his life" (Rom 5:10); "and you who were once estranged and hostile in mind, doing evil deeds" (Col 1:21); "for he [Christ] . . . has broken down the dividing wall, that is, the hostility between us. He has abolished the law with its commandments and ordinances" (Eph 2:14–15).

11. Rom 2:6; Heb 2:2.

12. "Therefore, just as sin came into the world through one man, and death came through sin, and so death spread to all because all have sinned" (Rom 5:12); "do not be deceived; God is not mocked" (Gal 6:7); "all of us . . . were by nature children of wrath" (Eph 2:3); "what should we say? That God is unjust to inflict wrath on us?" (Rom 3:5); "but by your hard and impenitent heart you are storing up wrath for yourself on

the day of wrath, when God's righteous judgment will be revealed" (Rom 2:5); "this is evidence of the righteous judgment of God . . . to repay with affliction those who afflict you, and to give relief to the afflicted as well as to us, when the Lord Jesus is revealed from heaven . . . in flaming fire, inflicting vengeance on those who do not know God and on those who do not obey the gospel . . . These will suffer the punishment of eternal destruction" (2 Thess 1:5–9); "I am of the flesh, sold into slavery under sin. I do not understand my own actions. For I do not do what I want, but I do the very thing I hate . . . it is no longer I that do it, but the sin that dwells within me. For I know that nothing good dwells within me, that is, in my flesh . . . For I delight in the law of God in my inmost self, but I see in my members another law at war with the law of my mind, making me captive to the law of sin that dwells in my members" (Rom 7:14–23).

13. "For the creation waits with eager longing for the revealing of the children of God; for the creation was subjected to futility, not of its own will but by the will of the one who subjected it, in hope that the creation itself will be set free from its bondage to decay and will obtain the freedom of the glory of the children of God. We know that the whole creation has been groaning in labor pains until now" (Rom 8:19–22).

14. "For just as by the one man's disobedience the many were made sinners, so by the one man's obedience the many will be made righteous" (Rom 5:19); "for if the many died through the one man's trespass, much more surely have the grace of God and the free gift in the grace of the one man, Jesus Christ, abounded for the many" (Rom 5:15).

15. "This world was made by God like some paradise as a single world which has been made incorruptible on the one hand, and material and sensible on the other . . . For that very reason Adam was created having an incorruptible body, although it was wholly material and not yet spiritual, and was set by God the Creator as an immortal king in an incorruptible world—I do not say only in paradise, but in the whole of the subcelestial realm" (Symeon the New Theologian, *Treatise* 1, in *Traités théologiques et éthiques* [Theological and ethical discourses], Sources Chrétiennes 122 [Paris: Cerf, 1966], 174, 184). "The difference between the constitution of the human body in our forebear Adam before the fall and the constitution observable and prevailing in us now . . . that is to say, with humanity up to that time not pulled apart by corruptible qualities opposed to each other according to the constitution of the body, but staying just the same without flow and counterflow, and being free of constant change with regard to both of these according to the prevailing state of the qualities of constant change, in such a way as to be by grace not without a share in immortality and not to possess the corruption which now afflicts us with its stings" (Maximus the Confessor, *Ambigua* [PG 91:1352–53a]).

16. See Theodor Zahn, *Das Evangelium des Matthäus*, 2nd ed., Kommentar zum Neuen Testament (Leipzig: Deichert, 1905). Leonidas Philippidis notes, "Genealogical tables possessed the character of public documents (see Josephus, *Life* 1)," clearly to ensure the leading social status of the priests, who in any case belonged to the tribe of Levi (*Istoria tēs epochēs tēs Kainēs Diathēkēs* [Athens, 1958], 437).

17. See J. G. Else and P. C. Lee, *Primate Evolution* (Cambridge: Cambridge University Press, 1986); D. R. Pilbeam, "The Earliest Hominids" and "Rethinking Human Origins," in *Primate Evolution and Human Origins*, ed. Russell L. Ciochon and John G. Fleagle (New York: Aldine de Gruyter, 1987); R. Lewin, *Human Evolution: An Illustrated Introduction* (New York: Freeman, 1984).

18. The differences are much greater in comparison with the earlier *Homo habilis* or *Homo erectus*, which clearly should be classified as species of evolved ape. See Terrence Deacon, *The Symbolic Species: The Co-Evolution of Language and the Human Brain* (London: Allen Lane, Penguin, 1997), 340–49; Misia Landau, *Narratives of Human Evolution* (New Haven, CT: Yale University Press, 1991), 111–12.

19. Thanks to advances in genetics, the principle of the *evolution of species* is understood today in a very different way from that which determined Darwin's theory. Darwin had no knowledge of the mechanisms of heredity. Today we know that what an organism transmits to its descendants through reproduction is its genes, that is to say, codified instructions, or "packets" of information. The need to adapt to the environment, the function of *natural selection*, can lead the individuals of a species not to create new information but only to "shed" genetic information, thus modifying the original stock of genes.

A population of plants, for example, has a certain number of genes that determine the size of the roots. Over a long period, if the plants come to be in a dry environment, those with the longest roots, a trait that allows them to draw up water and salts from a greater depth, will be the ones that survive. Thus the genes responsible for shorter roots have a lower chance of surviving and being inherited. After a certain period, none of the plants of this specific population will possess genes for short roots, because only the plants with long roots will have survived. The information for longer roots was in the genes of the ancestral population. Adaptation to the environment, or the working of *natural selection*, did not elicit new or additional information but reduced the amount of information. Those plants that became capable of surviving in a drier environment shed a part of the genetic information that the ancestral individuals of the species possessed; the price of adaptation is the definitive loss of information in these plants. If the plants' environment becomes wet again and smaller roots become indispensable for survival, the genetic information (or genes) for the smaller roots will not reappear, and that particular population will not be able to adapt to the new conditions.

This form of adaptation to the environment was regarded by Darwin as a process that functioned in an unlimited way and was thus the cause of significant variations in living organisms. Because in a relatively short time new varieties of a particular species can appear, in much longer periods of, say, millions of years, new taxonomic groups of species could be formed—birds could emerge from reptiles, amphibians from fish, and so forth.

With the discovery and study of the function of genes and the composition of DNA, such possibilities have been ruled out—the evolutionary transition from one species to another is not possible. This impossibility emerges simply from the application of statistical methods to the analysis of evolutionary possibilities (the methodology of mathematical molecular biology). The probability of transition from one species to another presupposes an inconceivably large number of synchronized, specialized changes in the genes, precisely coincidental but entirely chance codifications (DNA) of genetic information—chance mutations and chance new combinations of reproductive genes—such that not only the period of time life has existed on earth but even the whole history of the universe (about fifteen billion years) would not be sufficient for them to take place.

More specifically, for a new living organism to be born, certain aleatory, or "chance," changes take place in the genetic code, or DNA, of the 10^{10} nuclei that compose it. The changes are aleatory because only these are transmitted: acquired characteristics are not inherited—that is to say, they do not contribute new genetic information (if some animal loses an eye, this does not mean that some descendant will be born with only one eye). Aleatory changes create a new code, which determines new inheritable characteristics. If the new characteristics happen, again by chance, to be successful from the point of view of natural adaptation, then the new living organism that emerges will survive and with it, a new genetic code, or set of DNA. If the contrary is the case, both the organism and the code will disappear.

If we calculate how many such aleatory codes (DNA) must pass the test of natural selection so that life can evolve from single-cell organisms to human beings (as Darwinists would claim)—codes sufficiently stable and viable to constitute *links* in life's evolutionary chain—we can assert what was noted above, namely, that even the age of the universe provides an insufficient time span.

On the basis of mathematical molecular biology, a theory of the evolution of species on the basis of chance genetic changes, or trials, and control through natural selection does not seem scientifically valid today. Recourse to a synergistic operation of natural selection and pure chance calls more for a metaphysical than for a scientific line of research.

See John Brockman, *The Third Culture: Beyond the Scientific Revolution* (New York: Simon and Schuster, 1995); Manfred Eigen, *Steps Towards Life: A Perspective on Evolution* (New York: Oxford University Press, 1992); Lynn Margulis, *The Symbiotic Planet: A New Look at Evolution* (London: Weidenfeld and Nicolson, 1998); Lynn Margulis and Dorion Sagan, *Microcosmos: Four Billion Years of Evolution from Our Microbial Ancestors* (Berkeley: University of California Press, 1998); Daniel Dennett, *Darwin's Dangerous Idea: Evolution and the Meanings of Life* (New York: Simon and Schuster, 1995); George C. Williams, *Natural Selection: Domains, Levels and Challenges* (New York: Oxford University Press, 1992).

Chapter 18

1. See the more extensive discussion in Yannaras, *Meta-neōterikē meta-physikē*, Eng. trans. *Postmodern Metaphysics*, theses 2.1 and 2.2.

2. See Xavier Léon-Dufour, ed., *Vocabulaire de théologie biblique* (Paris: Cerf, 1974); Rudolf Bultmann, "Thanatos," in *Theologisches Wörterbuch zum Neuen Testament*, 10 vols., ed. G. Kittel and G. Friedrich (Stuttgart: Kohlhammer, 1933–79), 3:7ff.; and Bultmann, *Theologie des Neuen Testaments*, 4th ed. (Tübingen: Mohr, 1961), 246ff., 346ff.

3. W. Warnach, O. H. Pesch, and R. Spaemann, "Freiheit," in *Historisches Wörterbuch der Philosophie*, 12 vols., ed. J. Ritter (Basel: Schwabe, 1971–2005), 2:1064–98 (a comprehensive entry with a full bibliography).

4. See Sigmund Freud, "Das Unbewusste," in *Gesammelte Werke*, 10:280, 285–88, 294.

5. Jacques Lacan, "L'inconscient est structuré comme un langage," in *Le séminaire* 11:23; Lacan, *Écrits* 2:203.

6. Lacan, *Le séminaire* 11:27.

7. Ibid., 116.

8. Ibid., 226.

9. There is a somewhat fuller treatment of this in Yannaras, *Orthos logos kai koinōnikē kritikē*, 4, 2; see also Yannaras, *To rhēto kai to arrhēto*, chap. 15; and Yannaras, *Meta-neōterikē meta-physikē*, 102–3, 189–90, 220–23; Yannaras, *Postmodern Metaphysics*, 64–66, 135–36, 162–65.

Chapter 19

1. T. S. Eliot, *The Family Reunion*, toward the end of the first scene of the second part.

2. See Wilhelm Michaelis, *"Piptō-ptōma-ptōsis,"* in *Theologisches Wörterbuch zum Neuen Testament,* ed. G. Kittel (Stuttgart: Kohlhammer, 1933–1979), 6:161–74; Ulrich Dierse, "Fall, Abfall," in *Historisches Worterbuch der Philosophie,* 12 vols., ed. J. Ritter (Basel: Schwabe, 1971–2005), 2:887–94; Alfred Jeremias, *Die ausserbiblische Erlösererwartung,* Quellen Lebensbücherei christl. Zeugnisse aller Jh.e (Berlin, 1927); Alfred Forke, *Geschichte der Alten Chinesischen Philosophie* (Hamburg: Walter de Gruyter, 1927); M. Winternitz, *Geschichte der indischen Literatur,* 2 vols. (Leipzig, 1909 and 1920); J. Scheftelowitz, *Die altpersische Religion und das Judentum* (Giessen, 1920).

3. See Martin Heidegger, *Sein und Zeit* (Eng. trans. *Being and Time*), § 15; Christos Yannaras, *To prosōpo kai o erōs* (Eng. trans. *Person and Eros*), § 12.

4. See Lacan, *Le séminaire* 11:180.

5. See Yannaras, *To rhēto kai to arrhēto,* chap. 15.

6. *Todestriebe-Ichtriebe-Selbserhaltungstriebe*; see the explanation of these Freudian terms in J. Laplanche and J.-B. Pontalis, *Vocabulaire de la psychoanalyse.*

7. Ilias Papagiannopoulos, *Exodos theatrou: Dokimio ontologias me ploēgo ton "Moby Dick" tou H. Melville* (Athens: Indiktos, 2000), 108.

Chapter 20

1. A consistent naturalism not only refuses to attribute a pejorative sense of evil to the instinctive urges of self-preservation and the acquisition of power and domination, but also sees in the instinctive urges the real starting point or cause even of the manifestations of so-called (by logical contradistinction to evil) good. Such naturalism attributes to manifestations of natural-biological necessities and demands that which is signified by words such as *spirit, civilization, meaning of the existent, struggle for goals.* The following statements of Panagiotis Kondylis in his *Ischys kai apophasē* (Athens: Stigmi, 1991) are indicative: "The so-called 'spirit' . . . aims at being a curbing or transcending of instinctive urges, but only becomes a substitute or continuation of them" (143). "The transcendence of 'instinct' by means of 'spirit' finally serves the same 'instinct' . . . The functional weaknesses of 'instinct' gave birth to 'spirit' . . . 'Spirit' did not change in the slightest the basic givens in the pursuit of self-preservation, which in their basic lines are already determined by the biostructure" (146–48). "Within civilization, through civilization, and for the sake of civilization a transfer of nature to the ideal level takes place . . . Thus, for example, the sex drive is channeled into marriage or is idealized as erotic love; even murder is honored if it is committed for a 'just cause'" (89–90). "The pursuit of power takes

the form of a struggle for certain goals . . . From the side-road of faith, where a *meaning* is given to life, a critical transfer is made of the urge of self-preservation and the pursuit of power to the level of the ideal and the regulative . . . The urge of self-preservation in a civilized society is raised to the level of an ideal and is transformed into a belief about the meaning of life" (91–92).

It should be evident to the reader that in the present work theses such as those of Panagiotis Kondylis are presupposed both as posing the question and as issuing a challenge—not, however, as setting out aphoristic summaries.

2. "C'est la libido, en tant que pur instinct de vie, c'est-à-dire de vie immortelle, de vie irrépressible, de vie qui n'a besoin, elle, d'aucun or-gane, de vie simplifiée et indestructible" (Lacan, *Le séminaire* 11:180).

3. Maximus the Confessor, *Chapters on Theology* 2.1 (PG 90:1125a).

4. Gen 2:17.

5. Lacan, *Le séminaire* 11:181.

6. "Desidero, c'est le *cogito* freudien" (Lacan, *Le séminaire* 11:141).

7. For the relativity of the images of reality that the—in all other respects—incomparably marvelous functions of sight, hearing, speech, smell, and taste give us, the reader may consult any handbook of human physiology. Here I have relied on a textbook by Professor Michael Apos-tolakis of the Thessaloniki Medical School, *To neuriko systēma*, vol. 4 of Stoicheia physiologias tou anthrōpou (Thessaloniki: Kyriakidis, 1982). Among works in Western European languages, see A. Iggo, ed., *Hand-book of Sensory Physiology* (New York: Springer, 1973); R. L. Gregory, *Eye and Brain* (London: Weidenfeld and Nicolson, 1966); R. Jung, O. H. Gauer, and K. Kramer, eds., *Physiologie des Menschen* (Munich: Urban und Schwarzenberg, 1976).

8. From the Greek *ex-istamai, exō-istamai*, "to become separated from," "to stand out of."

9. See what I have said, especially about time, in Yannaras, *Sche-diasma eisagogēs stē philosophia* (French trans. *Philosophie sans rup-ture*), § 32: "If relation constitutes the *mode of existence*, then time or the *aeon* (in the sense that Plato gave the word) simply 'measure' the fact of relation, although they are constituted as experiences of it. The aeon can then be interpreted as the unquantifiable *now* of the fullness of the relation—where as *fullness of relation* we should understand the identity of the existential beginning and the existential end or goal, the self-realization of being, which can only be expressed as nonmovement, while it does not cease to constitute a referentiality of life of different hypostases, that is to say, to constitute *love (agapē)* as an ontological category (according to Maximus the Confessor, as 'ever-moving mo-tionlessness and stationary constant movement'). Accordingly, time can

then be interpreted as the moving *now*, that is to say, as a fact of relation that is constantly transferred to its fulfilling realization, and for this reason it ceaselessly annuls the unquantifiable character of the pleromatic present." (According to Maximus again: "The *aeon* is time when it ceases from movement, and time is the *aeon* when it is measured as carried forward by movement. So the *aeon* is time deprived of movement, time is the *aeon* measured by movement" [*Ambigua* (PG 91:1164bc)]).

10. Matt 10:30; see also Luke 12:6–7: "Are not five sparrows sold for two pennies? Yet not one of them is forgotten in God's sight. But even the hairs of your head are all counted. Do not be afraid; you are of more value than many sparrows."

11. 1 Cor 13:12.

Bibliography

Apostolakis, Michael. *To neuriko systēma*. Vol. 4 of Stoicheia physio-logias tou anthrōpou. Thessaloniki: Kyriakidis, 1982.

Babiniotis, Georgios D. *Lexiko tēs neas Ellēnikēs glōssas*. 3rd ed. Athens: Kentro Lexikologias, 2008.

Brockman, John. *The Third Culture: Beyond the Scientific Revolution*. New York: Simon and Schuster, 1995.

Bultmann, Rudolf. *"Thanatos."* In G. Kittel and G. Friedrich, eds., *Theologisches Wörterbuch zum Neuen Testament*, 3:7ff.

_____. *Theologie des Neuen Testaments*. 4th ed. Tübingen: Mohr, 1961. Translated as *Theology of the New Testament* (London: SCM Press, 1983).

Castoriadis, Cornelius. *The Imaginary Institution of Society*. Translated by Kathleen Blamey. Cambridge, MA: MIT Press, 1998.

Deacon, Terrence. *The Symbolic Species: The Co-Evolution of Language and the Human Brain*. London: Allen Lane, Penguin, 1997.

Dimitrakos, Dimitrios. *Mega lexikon holēs tēs Ellēnikēs glossēs*. 15 vols. Athens: Dimitrakos, Rebezikas, 1954–58.

Dennett, Daniel. *Darwin's Dangerous Idea: Evolution and the Meanings of Life*. New York: Simon and Schuster, 1995.

Diels, Hermann, trans., and Walther Kranz, ed. *Die Fragmente der Vorsokratiker*. 3 vols. Berlin: Weidmannsche Verlagsbuch-handlung, 1952.

Dierse, Ulrich. "Fall, Abfall." In *Historisches Worterbuch der*

Philosophie. 12 vols. Edited by J. Ritter, 2:887–94. Basel: Schwabe, 1971–2005.

Eccles, J. C. *How the Self Controls Its Brain*. Berlin: Springer Verlag, 1994.

Edelman, Gerald M. *Bright Air, Brilliant Fire: On the Matter of the Mind*. New York: Basic Books, 1992.

Eigen, Manfred. *Steps Towards Life: A Perspective on Evolution*. New York: Oxford University Press, 1992.

Einstein, Albert. *Mein Weltbild*. Berlin: Ullstein, 1934. Translated by Alan Harris as *The World as I See It* (London: Watts, 1940).

Else, J. G., and P. C. Lee, eds. *Primate Evolution*. Cambridge: Cambridge University Press, 1986.

Forke, Alfred. *Geschichte der Alten Chinesischen Philosophie*. Hamburg: Walter de Gruyter, 1927.

Freud, Sigmund. "Das Unbewusste." In *Gesammelte Werke*, vol. 10.

———. "Die sexuellen Abirrungen." In *Drei Abhandlungen zur Sexualtheorie*. Leipzig: Teschen, 1905. Translated by James Strachey as *Three Essays on the Theory of Sexuality* (London: Hogarth Press, 1962).

———. "Formulierungen über die zwei Prinzipien des psychischen Geschehens." In *Gesammelte Werke*, 8:230–38.

———. *Gesammelte Werke*. 18 vols. London: Imago, 1940–68.

———. *Jenseits des Lustprinzips*. Leipzig: Internationaler Psychoanalytischer Verlag, 1920. Translated by John Reddick as *Beyond the Pleasure Principle and Other Writings* (London: Penguin, 2003).

———. "Suggestion und Libido." In *Massenpsychologie und Ich-Analyse*. Leipzig: Internationaler Psychoanalytischer Verlag, 1921. Translated by James Strachey et al. as *Group Psychology and the Analysis of the Ego* (New York: Bantam Books, 1960).

Gregory, R. L. *Eye and Brain*. London: Weidenfeld and Nicolson, 1966.

Heidegger, Martin. *Sein und Zeit*. Halle: Niemayer, 1927. Translated by John Macquarrie and Edward Robinson as *Being and Time* (London: SCM Press, 1962).

Iggo, A., ed. *Handbook of Sensory Physiology*. New York: Springer, 1973.

Isaac the Syrian. *Oration 67*. In *Ascetical Works*. Leipzig, 1770. Reprint, Athens: Ch. Spanos, n.d.

Jeremias, Alfred. *Die ausserbiblische Erlösererwartung*. Quellen Lebensbücherei christlicher Zeugnisse aller Jahrhundert. Berlin, 1927.

John Damascene. *Dialectica.* Edited by Bonifatius Kotter. Berlin: Walter de Gruyter, 1969.

Johnson, Mark. *The Body in the Mind: The Bodily Basis of Meaning, Imagination and Reason.* Chicago: University of Chicago Press, 1987.

Jung, R., O. H. Gauer, and K. Kramer, eds. *Physiologie des Menschen.* Munich: Urban und Schwarzenberg, 1976.

Kittel, G., and G. Friedrich. *Theologisches Wörterbuch zum Neuen Testament.* 10 vols. Stuttgart: Kohlhammer, 1933–79.

Kondylis, Panagiotis. *Ischys kai apophasē.* Athens: Stigmi, 1991.

Lacan, Jacques. *Écrits*, vol. 2. Paris: Seuil, 1971.

_____. "Les formations de l'inconscient." *Bulletin de Psychologie* 2 (1957–58): 1–15.

_____. *Le séminaire de Jacques Lacan.* Livre 11. Paris: Seuil, 1973.

_____. "L'inconscient est structuré comme un langage." In *Le séminaire de Jacques Lacan*, 11:23.

_____. "Subversion du sujet et dialectique du désir dans l'inconscient freudien." In *Écrits* 2:151–91. Paris: Seuil, 1971.

Landau, Misia. *Narratives of Human Evolution.* New Haven, CT: Yale University Press, 1991.

Laplanche, J., and J.-B. Pontalis. *Vocabulaire de la psychanalyse.* 7th ed. Paris: Presses universitaires de France, 1981. Translated into English as *The Language of Psychoanalysis* (London: Hogarth Press, 1983) and into Greek as *Lexilogio tēs Psychanalysēs* (Athens: Kedros, 1986).

Léon-Dufour, Xavier, ed. *Vocabulaire de théologie biblique.* Paris: Cerf, 1974. Translated by P. J. Cahill as *Dictionary of Biblical Theology* (London: Burns and Oates, 2004).

Lewin, R. *Human Evolution: An Illustrated Introduction.* New York: Freeman, 1984.

Margulis, Lynn. *The Symbiotic Planet: A New Look at Evolution.* London: Weidenfeld and Nicolson, 1998.

Margulis, Lynn, and Dorion Sagan. *Microcosmos: Four Billion Years of Evolution from Our Microbial Ancestors.* Berkeley: University of California Press, 1998.

McCulloch, W. S. *Embodiments of Mind.* Cambridge, MA: MIT Press, 1989.

Michaelis, Wilhelm. "*Piptō-ptōma-ptōsis*." In G. Kittel and G. Friedrich, eds., *Theologisches Wörterbuch zum Neuen Testament*, 6:161–74.

Monk, Ray. *Ludwig Wittgenstein: The Duty of Genius*. London: Jonathan Cape, 1990.

Papagiannopoulos, Ilias. *Exodos theatrou: Dokimio ontologias me ploēgo ton* Moby Dick *tou H. Melville*. Athens: Indiktos, 2000.

Penrose, Roger. *The Large, the Small and the Human Mind*. Cambridge: Cambridge University Press, 1997.

Philippidis, Leonidas. *Istoria tēs epochēs tēs Kainēs Diathēkēs*. Athens, 1958.

Pilbeam, D. R. "The Earliest Hominids" and "Rethinking Human Origins." In *Primate Evolution and Human Origins*, edited by Russell L. Ciochon and John G. Fleagle. New York: Aldine de Gruyter, 1987.

Pinker, Steven. *Language Learnability and Language Development*. Cambridge, MA: Harvard University Press, 1984.

Plotinus. *Enneads*. Translated by A. H. Armstrong. 6 vols. Loeb Classic Library. Cambridge, MA: Harvard University Press, 1966–88.

Popper, Karl. *Logik der Forschung*. Tübingen: J. C. Mohr, 1982. Translated as *The Logic of Scientific Discovery* (London: Routledge, 1992).

Putnam, Hilary. *Representation and Reality*. Cambridge, MA: MIT Press, 1988.

Ramfos, Stelios. *O kaēmos tou enos*. Athens: Armos, 2000. Translated by Norman Russell as *Yearning for the One* (Brookline, MA: Holy Cross Orthodox Press, 2011).

Scheftelowitz, J. *Die altpersische Religion und das Judentum*. Giessen, 1920.

Searle, John. *Minds, Brains, and Science*. Cambridge, MA: Harvard University Press, 1984.

Shepherd, Gordon M. *Neurobiology*. New York: Oxford University Press, 1983.

Symeon the New Theologian. *Treatise* 1. In *Traités théologiques et éthiques* [Theological and ethical treatises]. Sources Chrétiennes 122. Edited by J. Darrouzès. Paris: Cerf, 1966.

Vasse, Denis. *Le temps du désir*. Paris: Seuil, 1969.

Warnach, W., O. H. Pesch, and R. Spaemann. "Freiheit." In *Historisches Wörterbuch der Philosophie*, 2:1964–98. Edited by J. Ritter. Basel: Schwabe, 1972.

Williams, George C. *Natural Selection: Domains, Levels and Challenges*. New York: Oxford University Press, 1992.

Winternitz, M. *Geschichte der indischen Literatur*. 2 vols. Leipzig, 1909 and 1920.

Wittgenstein, Ludwig. *Tractatus logico-philosophicus*. Translated by D. F. Pears and B. F. McGuinness. London: Routledge, 2001.

_____. *Philosophical Grammar*. Edited by Rush Rhees and translated by Anthony Kenny. Oxford: Blackwell, 1974.

Yannaras, Christos. *E apanthrōpia tou dikaiōmatos*. Athens: Domos, 1998.

_____. *Heidegger kai Areopagitēs*. 4th ed. Athens: Domos, 1998. Translated by Haralambos Ventis as *On the Absence and Unknowability of God: Heidegger and the Areopagite* (London: T&T Clark International, 2005).

_____. *Meta-neōterikē meta-physikē*. Athens: Domos, 1993. Translated by Norman Russell as *Postmodern Metaphysics* (Brookline, MA: Holy Cross Orthodox Press, 2004).

_____. *Orthos logos kai koinōnikē praktikē*. 2nd ed. Athens: Domos, 1990.

_____. *Protaseis kritikēs ontologias*. 3rd ed. Athens: Domos, 1995.

_____. *Schediasma eisagōgēs stē philosophia*. 4th ed. Athens: Domos, 1994. Translated by André Borrély as *Philosophie sans rupture* (Geneva: Labor et Fides, 1998).

_____. *To pragmatiko kai to phantasiōdes stēn politikē oikonomia*. 2nd ed. Athens: Domos, 1966.

_____. *To prosōpo kai o erōs*. Athens: Domos, 1976. Translated by Norman Russell as *Person and Eros* (Brookline, MA: Holy Cross Orthodox Press, 2008).

_____. *To rhēto kai to arrhēto: Ta glōssika oria realismou tēs metaphysikēs*. Athens: Ikaros, 1999.

Zahn, Theodor. *Das Evangelium des Matthäus*. 2nd ed. Kommentar zum Neuen Testament. Leipzig: Deichert, 1905.

Index